THE GLORY OF GROVELING

Apology: a Simple Path to More Freedom and Happiness

THE GLORY OF GROVELING

Apology: a Simple Path to More Freedom and Happiness

Skyhorse Publishing

Skyhorse Publishing books may be purchased in bulk at special discounts for sales promotion, corporate gifts, fund-raising, or educational purposes. Special editions can also be created to specifications. For details, contact the Special Sales Department, Skyhorse Publishing, 307 Fifth Avenue, 4th Floor, New York, NY 10016 or info@skyhorsepublishing.com.

Visit our website at www.skyhorsepublishing.com.

10 9 8 7 6 5 4 3 2 1

Library of Congress Cataloging-in-Publication Data is available on file.

Cover design by David Ter-Avanesyan and Jason Feddy
Cover photo credit: Getty Images

Print ISBN: 978-1-5107-8527-4
Ebook ISBN: 978-1-5107-8529-8

Printed in the United States of America

To our loving families and especially to our wives, Ava Burton and Cindy Waldman, for their incredible patience and forgiveness, always.

TABLE OF CONTENTS

A NOTE FROM THE AUTHORS

Human beings are social animals. All of our connections and interactions are integral to the fabric of life. Very few of us are reclusive or solitary people. We need each other, and our relationships largely shape who we are and the quality of our lives.

We (the authors) have written a short book for everyone who has any type of relationship with anyone. It is designed for people who are in love (or have been or plan to be in love), for those with families and friends, and for people who work with other people. It is a book for you.

Among other things, this book contains a simple yet powerful way to use a skillful apology as a tool to mend broken relationships. This book will teach you how to apologize skillfully, how to be accountable for yourself, and how to create more freedom and happiness in your life and others.

However, we are aware that sometimes people find themselves in very dangerous situations that fall outside of the scope of this book.

If you are suffering from physical or mental or emotional abuse, the authors strongly recommend that you swiftly seek professional advice, be it medical, psychological, legal or otherwise.

FOREWORDS

Why Your Next Apology Could Save Your Life

Picture this: You're carrying around fifty pounds of invisible weight—the accumulated burden of every unresolved conflict, every broken relationship, every time you were too proud to say "I'm sorry." Now imagine setting that weight down with six and a half carefully crafted steps.

Jason Feddy and Michael Waldman's *The Glory of Groveling* presents apology not as weakness but as neurological transformation. When you genuinely apologize—acknowledging what you did, how you were being, and making specific promises for the future—your brain literally rewires itself. My reading of the research is stunning: effective apologies trigger measurable changes in stress hormones and activate the same neural networks involved in empathy and emotional regulation.

The book is a unique synthesis of 12-Step wisdom, executive coaching, and phenomenological philosophy.

The title, "The Glory of Groveling," is deliberately provocative. "Groveling" suggests humiliation, submission, loss of dignity. But Feddy and Waldman reclaim the word, finding glory in the very act that seems most degrading. They're following Shakespeare, who coined "grovel" in *Henry VI* using it to describe someone brought low—but also brought to earth, grounded, made real.

This surprising definition connects to a deeper philosophy: we are all "perfectly imperfect." It is not a new-age consolation but rather a clear-eyed recognition of reality. You're going to make mistakes, not because you're broken but because you're human. The question isn't *whether* you'll hurt people—it's whether you'll have the courage to make it right.

And your willingness to own your mistakes, to sit in that uncomfortable café with someone you've wronged, to promise specific behavioral changes—that's what transforms neural pathways and relationships.

— **Joe Ferguson PhD/MBA**, clinical psychologist, philosopher, and writer

The Glory of What???

I have known Jason Feddy for ten years, and I had no idea he was this smart. I don't know his collaborator, Michael Waldman; he said "hello" to me in the street yesterday and then, for some unknown reason, he immediately apologized.

Since I failed to wear the reading glasses I always need when I began reading the book, I first thought it was called "The Glory of Gravelling," and this made no sense to me. I put on my glasses and it immediately began to make better sense. Everyone who has ever had a broken relationship should read this book. I am now going to grovel to my piano teacher for not practicing. I was only six, but I've been hanging on to it; this book will help me let it go.

—**Rita Rudner**, American stand-up comedian and actress.

ABOUT THE AUTHORS

Jason Feddy is a British-American musician, songwriter, radio personality, and teacher. He was the 2019–20 Laguna Beach Arts Alliance "Artist of The Year" and is a passionate collaborator with a number of local arts organizations. For a decade, Jason was a cantor/soloist (song and service leader) for Temple Isaiah of Newport Beach, California, and currently provides music for The Jewish Collaborative of Orange County. He is a consultant for the Cultural Arts Department of Laguna Beach, curating many of the city's numerous outdoor music programs, and is a board member at Laguna Beach Cultural Arts Center.

As a songwriter, Jason has made eight albums of original songs, and his music has been featured on soundtracks for movies. His most recent collection, "Songs from the Plays," features lyrics by William Shakespeare, all set to Jason's modern, acoustic music. Jason wrote the songs, performed in, and was musical director for the off-Broadway show *Two's A Crowd*, written by and starring comedian Rita Rudner. In the *New York Times* review of the show, Jason was described as having embodied "Rumpled Charm."

Over the years, Feddy has been in and has led more bands than he can remember, from trios to nine-piece extravaganzas. He's still friends with everyone in those bands, even the drummers. He travels the world talking and singing to anyone who will listen.

A former heroin addict, Jason has been clean and sober by way of a 12-Step program since 2000. By his own account he has fucked up so many times over the years, sober or not, that he's put in way more than his 10,000 hours of practice in the art of apology; learning along the way. Jason has helped many people to fix broken relationships, based on his knowledge and experience of the 12 Steps, particularly Steps 8 and 9—the preparation and making of "amends." Due to many years of honest apologies and rarely broken promises, he is very close with his numerous family members, who live across three continents.

Jason's fabulous wife Ava, who knew him at his worst, married him in 2010, and it is by apologizing so well that they have avoided strangling each other. They have a little white dog, Barklee, who loves them both very much.

Michael Waldman, at seventy, has spent his professional life as a teacher, thought leader, entrepreneur, and trusted business consultant focused on his clients' extraordinary accomplishments and personal satisfaction.

Michael was a founding partner of two global management consulting companies, High Performance Consulting and Insigniam Consulting—specializing in Strategic Design, Breakthrough Performance, and Leadership Development for the Fortune Global 100. These consulting companies and their clients have allowed Michael to consult throughout Asia, Europe, South America, and North America.

Michael has been acknowledged or quoted in the books, *The Three Laws of Performance* and *Take Time for Your Life*. His perspective is that in business, it all comes down to the human factor, the people. Simply said, it's impossible to have unprecedented business results unless your team is inspired, self-expressed, aligned, and unstoppably productive.

Prior to starting his consulting companies, Michael was a senior course leader for Landmark Worldwide, a global education corporation. During this time, Michael worked with thousands of individuals on their most important personal and business issues, including improving relationships, building personal communication skills, being more confident and productive, clearing away self-limitations, and designing inspiring futures for themselves.

Long committed to social contribution, Michael was a founding board member and Chairman of the Board of the Somaly Mam Foundation, an anti-human-trafficking non-profit organization. He has also consulted the American Red Cross, the Boy Scouts of America, and the Laguna Beach Festival of the Arts.

Today, Michael lives in Laguna Beach, CA, with his wife Cindy and enjoys time with their son and daughter-in-law. He is an iPhone photographer, and his photos have been published in Steven Van Zandt's album *Soulfire Live!* and his book *Unrequited Infatuations*. Additionally, his photography is seen in Robert Lawson's *Solidarity Forever*. His love for music has led him to appear in movies about Cream and Bruce Springsteen. The Grammy

Museum featured an interview with Michael in its Springsteen Live exhibit film.

Along with writing with Jason, he devotes his time to providing executive coaching for a small number of corporate clients on performance, leadership, and personal satisfaction.

Introduction

A Friend's Interaction with Jason.

Jason: My friend and I got a book deal.
Friend: Huh? What's it about?
Jason: It's called *The Glory of Groveling: Apology, a Simple Path to More Freedom and Happiness.*
Friend: Oh . . .
Jason: What do you think, do you fancy a little freedom and happiness?
Friend: Sure, but I wouldn't *grovel* for it.

We know, no one wants to *grovel.* It smacks of humiliation, submission, degradation, and worse. Fear not: you haven't picked up a book that intends to punch you in the mouth. There's nothing here to hurt you.

If you are sensing that we use the word, "groveling" as a joke, you are correct, but like most jokes, it contains a morsel of truth. Perhaps the prospect of apology sounds humiliating to you. Welcome, you are among friends.

One definition of "grovel" is "to humble oneself, as in making apologies or showing respect." As we'll see, being humble and being *humiliated* are two very different things.

In any case, the word "grovel," was coined by none other than William Shakespeare, a name you'll see scattered around this book in an attempt to make us look intelligent. As well as the commonly understood meaning—obsequious brown-nosing—Shakespeare used the word to mean what modern psychologists refer to as the right-sizing of the ego: being grounded in who we really are, how we really behave, and the actual effects we have on others.

In Shakespeare's *Henry IV Part 2*, Eleanor advises the Duke of Gloucester to grovel, to humble himself, until he wears the crown he seeks.

> **Eleanor:** ". . . What seest thou there? King
> Henry's diadem,
> Enchased with all the honours of the world?
> If so, gaze on, and *grovel* on thy face,
> Until thy head be circled with the same."

Clearly here, Eleanor is not counseling the Duke to humiliate himself, but rather to humble himself in order to attain the position he seeks.

WHY BOTHER?

"Listen: if I were alone in this world, I would have the right to choose despair, solitude and self-fulfillment. But I am not alone."

—Elie Wiesel

". . . from error to error one discovers the entire truth."

—Sigmund Freud

If you sit on a couch all day and never talk to anyone, you won't need this book.

If, however, you've ever had a job, been to school, been part of a family or had a friend, joined a club, stood in line, taken a cab, been on a date, or had a pizza delivered—if you've ever been in a romantic relationship with someone other than yourself, then you've engaged in some of the countless ways that human beings interact with one another. If this is you, then you've almost certainly made a few *mistakes* along the way.

This is likely to be especially true when it comes to the people you are closest to—the people with whom you interact frequently—your family, friends, and colleagues, your loved ones—the people in your life who are the most important to you. In spite of the fact that these relationships are often our most significant, we often make mistakes that put them in jeopardy. And, perhaps *because* these people are so essential to us, the impact of our mistakes can seem mystifying, hard to see and hard to resolve.

Take it from us, we are all *mistake-making machines*, and those mistakes come in an infinite number of shapes and sizes, from a tiny, innocuous word out of place, to accidentally stapling your mother's foot to the floor, to lying about your boss's halitosis. The spectrum can stretch through to something really mean done on purpose or much, much worse.

> Whatever the case, unless cleaned up and resolved, it is so often these every day, commonly made mistakes can lead to the death of a relationship—or place it on life-support—leaving it no longer satisfying or fulfilling.

When this happens we often describe those relationships as "difficult," or "complicated," or even "toxic," and we may say our friends are being "overly sensitive" or even "impossible." The bottom line is we don't feel as happy or free in those relationships as we would like. Not free. Not happy. Not good. Perhaps we don't feel as able to express ourselves—we don't feel able to say what's on our minds. Maybe we find ourselves feeling irritated or discontented. We may even think we have grown to *hate* the person in question. There is a wide range of how a broken relationship might look and how it can affect us, from mild discomfort in being around a person, to stink-eye in the workplace, all the way to big dramas that wind up in courtrooms or hospitals.

More than likely, each of us at some point has had someone in our life with whom our relationship is at least a little broken, someone we'd avoid at a party or dodge to the next aisle at the market if we spotted them. Many of us also have had people in our lives who we've wished would fall off a cliff. For the most part, however, the dissatisfaction we feel with those friends, acquaintances, and family members falls somewhere in between avoiding them and wanting to strangle them.

> **Consider this: It may not be obvious at first, but this discomfort is a clear sign of a broken relationship.**

This lack of freedom and happiness is simply *how we know*. So, the measure by which we ask you to judge whether you have a broken relationship is to ask yourself: Would I be happy to go to dinner with them sometime? Am I interested in their life? Could I look them in the eye and honestly smile, or would I rather they fall down a big hole? Does the idea of being around them leave me feeling uncomfortable? Am I happy—am I free in their presence?

When things go wrong between people, it is often very painful and disorienting. Feelings can be hurt, and people can become angry, resentful, sad, anxious, or even depressed. One's health can be affected. In business relationships, livelihoods can be threatened. Additionally, the effects of broken relationships aren't always just personal; they can spread out like ripples on a pond where innocent people become caught in the emotional undertow. This is why your sister-in-law stopped talking to you after you had an argument with your wife.

But don't just listen to us, look at yourself. How are you left when you've done something that upsets someone you care for? How are *you* when someone you care for does something that upsets you? Does it impact your sense of well-being? Does it affect your family or your work? Probably it is pretty miserable.

Boy, You're Gonna Carry That Weight

We assert—and have our own experiences to prove—that most people are trudging through life, carrying the weight of these broken and unresolved relationships.

Well, what does *that* mean?

Imagine the impossible: overnight you gained fifty pounds. How might that affect your day? All of sudden your knees and your back hurt, you are more tired, you are clumsier and more likely to bump into things and people than the day before. And if that isn't enough, here's the bad part: you get used to it all. It becomes the new normal, invisible.

Obviously nobody ever actually gained fifty pounds overnight, but people *have* lost relationships that quickly.

When it comes to broken and unresolved relationships, the added weight we carry is the resignation, dissatisfaction, and the stress that replaces the happiness and freedom we previously had.

We become irritable, and that which made us happy yesterday doesn't seem to work today.

That weight is there from the moment we wake up until bedtime. It becomes such a part of us that we hardly notice it. We do notice, however, that we are more tired, or less happy, or that we aren't thinking or listening clearly. Maybe we've lost our sense of humor, have become more cynical, or are just plain grumpy. When asked why this is, we may look for a reason and we may find one that we believe in, but we certainly don't see the actual connection between our malaise and a broken relationship. It's that invisible.

And a word about health: physical, emotional, and mental. The shelves of the self-help and medical sections of every bookstore are chock-full of writings on the connections between stress and poor health. Our own personal experience has shown us that the weight and stress of un-mended relationships can cause and perpetuate problems in the body and of the mind.

Our bet is that you've had your own experience with the impact of stress on your health. Commonly, people talk about the real physical impact of stress on medical issues like blood pressure, migraines, asthma, panic attacks, depression, etc. In fact, the definition of a psychosomatic illness includes the phrases stress-related and stress-induced.

And again, all of this quickly becomes the new normal—invisible to us, commonplace, and unremarkable. In this state, we just feel the way we feel and we don't know why. When asked how we're doing, we say things like, "It is what it is" and we're "hanging in there".

We can't see what got us here. And if it don't look broke, we don't fix it.

When in that state of mind, *if we don't make things right*, we are much more likely to make mistakes; the weight gets heavier, the cycle goes around and around, and our lives become a disaster!

OK, maybe not a *disaster*, but perhaps you can begin to see what we mean about unresolved relationships and the weight of their impact on our lives.

As experienced and effective apologizers, we know all of this is not inevitable; people do not have to suffer in this way. Here's the good news: *any* broken relationship we desire to be fixed can be fixed. The power to make things right again, to restore our freedom and happiness in our relationships, lies in a simple process that is in our hands. The emotional weight of broken relationships can be shed as quickly as it was added.

Simply said, each of us loses a sense of freedom and happiness as a result of the unresolved mistakes that cause relationships to deteriorate. *The Glory of Groveling* is a recipe for apologizing effectively to restore the sense of freedom and happiness lost in broken relationships.

You'd be forgiven for wondering: apologize? Say I'm wrong? To that bastard? Are you kidding? Surely they should be apologizing to me. Of course, I wish things were better between us, but I really didn't do anything wrong, and I can't see what they are so upset about.

Apologize? Yes, as a path to resolving those relationships. Give us a chapter or two to demonstrate how apologizing to those "bastards" will restore *your* sense of freedom and happiness. **At this stage, we ask you to open your mind to the idea that your definition of an apology is not the same as ours.** If you're not convinced, you can have your misery back in full later.

We, the authors, are not MDs or PhDs in the social sciences. Each of us has, however, dedicated decades of our lives, each in our own traditions, to studying, practicing, and supporting others in these ideas of apology. This book is a synthesis of all those years of learning and teaching.

As a result, we have become ordinary people with a rather large commitment to cleaning up our own messes and supporting others to do the same. Frankly, we're obsessed with it. It's not just something we talk about; it's in our bones. We're not young chaps—we have made many, many mistakes, and we've had the opportunity to make many, many apologies. We have noticed the impact of both the mistakes and the apologies on us and the people around us. We've seen the freedom and happiness that it brings. And this is what we've discovered . . .

An effective apology is as close to real magic as we have ever seen.

When practiced, an effective apology fixes broken relationships and allows them to flourish, or die if necessary, in a way that is complete and without shame. It dramatically reduces recovery time in arguments, it destroys the need for our defensiveness and passive-aggressive behavior, and it reduces our desire for what people commonly call "personal boundaries."

When it comes to stress-induced poor health, an apology reduces the stress so we might experience tangible relief. **Apology gives us the authority to determine our own future, free of the fear, resentment, and guilt we inherit from broken relationships. It makes us people of our word, people who can be trusted, people who are ready for real love.** We not only accept ourselves, our friends, and life itself with all its warts, but we actually become fascinated with the flawed nature of it all. And that is about 1 percent of what we mean by freedom and happiness.

In a 1972 interview for *Playboy* Magazine, world-renowned problem solver, designer, and philosopher Buckminster Fuller explained the symbolic value of the "Trim-tab." Imagine a huge ocean liner. Now, picture the enormous rudder that steers the boat. This rudder is controlled by a small component called a trim-tab—a tiny mini-rudder that provides enough pressure to shift the many thousands of tons that a liner weighs, to turn the ship around.

Restoring our sense of freedom and happiness can seem like a big ship to turn, but a well-executed apology is a trim-tab. An effective apology is a tiny device, which weighs and costs very little, but it can release thousands of pounds of emotional weight.

Imagine life without that weight. Imagine a life with no broken or unresolved relationships. Imagine all that, without too much trouble, by thoroughly and effectively apologizing.

Welcome to the Glory of Groveling.

Part One: The Steps

"You don't have to see the whole staircase, just take the first step."

— Martin Luther King, Jr.

"He who wants honey must endure the sting of bees."

— Arabic proverb

We are about to lay out before you, in as simple and direct a way as we can, a strategy for a successful apology.

Think of this book as a recipe for a great dish. In all recipes, there is a list of ingredients and a method for combining and cooking them. If you didn't know and we told you the recipe for an omelet was three eggs and a handful of mushrooms and left it at that, you'd be likely to create something other than an omelet. The eggs are vital, but it's the method that turns them into an omelet. The method for efficient and effective apology *is the entire book.*

In other words, don't miss out on a great meal, or a great relationship, by missing something in the recipe.

We have one more strong suggestion for you before you launch into these steps: find yourself what the science-fiction writer Robert A. Heinlein called a "Fair Witness," someone who can support you by bringing impartiality and confidentiality to your process. Pick someone who doesn't buy your bullshit, someone who isn't afraid of hitting you on the nose with a rolled-up newspaper. It is likely that your Fair Witness will see something crucial that you may have missed in your preparation. After all, we all have blind spots.

There is another key to having your Fair Witness actually make a difference. You will need to put aside your perspective and listen carefully to their thoughts. If you act on your own "conventional wisdom," you're likely to have a conventional outcome. If that's what you're looking for, you don't need a Fair Witness, or this book.

The humility it takes to find a Fair Witness and listen to them will serve you well as you follow the Six and a Half Steps.

One more note before we start the work to be done: we have named the person to whom you are going to apologize, your "Friend," though they may be your husband, wife, boss, child, or mortal enemy. We love irony as much as anyone, but this is not meant as a joke. The reasons this person is your Friend will become clear as we move on.

Step One:

Know and Own Your Mistakes

Step Two:

Ask Permission to Apologize

Step Three:

Say "I Am Really Sorry"

Step Four:

Admit the Impact of Your Mistake on Them

Step Five:

Promise You Can Be Trusted in the Future

Step Six:

Ask If You Can Do Anything More

Step Six and a Half:

Don't Push It

Step One: Know and Own Your Mistakes

So, you're a human being living in a world full of relationships with people at work, at home, and in your community. Naturally, you've made a few mistakes. It's completely normal that some of your relationships may be stuck or are staggering along without creating much in the way of freedom or happiness.

On the other hand, at the bleeding edge of the spectrum, you may have a relationship with a Friend in which communication has completely broken down. Wherever you are on this spectrum, it's on your mind and you want things to be better.

Right now, it's entirely possible and completely understandable if you can't see a connection between any mistake you have made and the breakdowns in your relationships. It's even possible you see the mistakes your Friend made more clearly than you see your own.

> No matter: whether you see it now or not, a successful Step One is about YOU discovering and owning how the actions YOU have taken have given rise to the current, shall we say, can-of-worms. It's your apology, not theirs.

A word about what we mean by ownership of your actions. Ownership points to that which belongs to you. And really, is there anything that belongs more closely to you than the things you say and the actions you take? Yet almost daily we blame those things on the traffic, the weather, our parents, the soccer results, the pizza we had for lunch, God, the butterfly effect, Sir Walter Raleigh, and anything else we can think of.

Why do we do this? To defend ourselves. To demonstrate that we aren't bad people. We want to be let off the hook. We don't want to be known as wrong or foolish or mean. Surely we're good people who are just victims of our circumstances. We're convinced that if only our Friends had the full picture, if they only knew what was in our hearts, our intentions and motivations, they would better understand and maybe even forgive us. While this reflex seems right, it's actually childlike. Why? Our knee-jerk reactions are often out of step with what's actually going on. Ultimately, as adults, folks judge us on what we do and say, not what we think or what's in our hearts.

This may appear harsh, but our experience tells us that our Friends don't really buy into our reasons and excuses—they only want us to take responsibility for our actions. At the end of the day, our Friends see what we did and the only way to restore that relationship is to flat-out apologize without trying to look good with a sincere excuse.

After all, your doctor doesn't really care why you didn't take your medication; they only care that you didn't take your medication and that your blood pressure is still dangerously high. And by the way, your blood pressure doesn't care why you didn't take your medication either.

It's *Your* Can of Worms

Now, let's pick a stuck relationship, your can of worms, and get started.

Start by telling your Fair Witness what happened, the whole story . . . what you did, what they did, all the circumstances, everything.

Michael says: I first did a Landmark Worldwide educational course in 1979. A fundamental and very powerful distinction in Landmark's programs is "the story versus what happened." This idea has made a significant positive difference in all of my relationships.

As you begin to think back over the situation, you will see that you have a narrative or a chronicle—an account of what happened. At first blush that account seems to be an accurate representation of what happened. What may be hidden from view is this account is just *your* recollection, mixed in with the feelings you have about it, your explanation of it all, and the decisions you've made since it happened. Furthermore, whether your account is accurate or not, even if you believe it is entirely factual, thoughtful, compassionate, and selfless, it is still only your story. *It belongs only to you and to no one else.* It's your account, and anyone involved will also have an account that is entirely theirs.

Furthermore, everyone's tale includes actions taken by heroes and villains, along with a set of explanations and reasons about why what happened, happened.

Interestingly, in your account the hero is usually you and the villain is usually someone else. Your tale is full of your good deeds and intentions. This is also true of the personal account of anyone involved, especially your Friend.

> We're just suggesting that most of your narrative isn't useful in restoring the relationship because it only exists where *you* are, in *your* thoughts and feelings, not where your Friend is, in their experience of what happened.

This will ultimately prevent you from really understanding your Friend and their perspective and will become very important as we move forward.

Your perspective is always subjective, and your memory is not always reliable.

We're not saying you're necessarily embellishing the facts or lying about what happened. It really doesn't matter how accurately you recall the events because in this context, your narrative is neither true nor false. It's just yours. We have no wish to belittle your feelings or your recollections; we are, however, saying that in an apology, they aren't that useful. In fact, they can be a burden.

Why aren't they that useful? Why can they be a burden?

Because you and I would probably fight to the death about whose account is right. This fight just perpetuates the break in the relationship and fixes nothing. Everyone walks away exhausted, feeling like shit, and even more justified than before.

So, if we are correct in stating that most of our narrative is useless, how do we determine what *is* useful?

Do this: take out the explanations, the whys, the feelings, and the what-*they*-did from your story and just focus on *what you did* or *did not do.*

Remember to ask your Fair Witness to help you to see this clearly. To separate your narrative from "What You Did."

Now do what you need to do to fully own this new and crucial perspective: ***Your* actions, and nothing else, gave rise to *your* can of worms.** To do this you will need to be deeply honest with yourself and not shy away from any part of the truth regarding what you did or did not do.

(Please remember our important caveat about victims of abuse at the beginning of the book.)

But, but, but, what about what they did? This is a very common and understandable response to the cringing feeling of only focusing on one's own actions or lack of them. We get it. It's uncomfortable and your thoughts or memories or judgments about what-they-did won't magically disappear. The tendency to fall back on them as a source of comfort is strong, but you already know that endlessly stirring up these feelings by "mulling over" what they did hasn't worked. Many of us have tried the "what about them" method for decades to no avail: it just made things worse. Our Friend's actions became more hurtful and ours more innocent until the poison of our feelings toward them just made us lonelier and more bitter. On the other hand, it got us to where we are today—ready to try something new. Pain is often the touchstone of growth.

Again, we want to stress that coming face to face with what we did is at the heart and soul of the Six and a Half Steps.

Is *this* perspective true? Who knows. What matters is that it works. This perspective is useful in restoring the relationship, along with your own freedom and happiness in it (including the joyous freedom to worry about what's a true perspective, and what isn't, without tying yourself up in knots).

The shedding of an old narrative in favor of a new unproven perspective can be disturbing. If it does unsettle you, notice that and carry on. In this way, in spite of the discomfort we're experiencing, we are really beginning to own what we have done.

The way to accomplish this step is to discuss it with your Fair Witness. Culturally, as human beings, we are so embedded in our own account that it's very difficult, if not impossible, to free ourselves from it without help.

Your knowledge and ownership of your behavior is your only goal. You'll know you've done it right when you suddenly relax and breathe out in the way that tells you you've let go of the drama, the righteousness, and the attachment you had to your narrative.

So, what exactly *did* you do? Simply put, finding this out is the real work of Step One.

Step Two: Ask Permission to Apologize

Even now, less than a third of the way through six and a half very detailed and counterintuitive steps to restoring freedom and happiness in a relationship, you have already come a long way. You have taken responsibility for your words and actions, and you have discussed them with a Fair Witness. But now, the rubber is about to hit the road; you are about to approach the person who has occupied your thoughts for some time. Shit, in other words, is about to get real.

You are probably feeling nervous or uncomfortable at the idea of approaching your Friend. What are you going to say? How will they respond? How will you both be left feeling afterward? Will the situation get worse? We have a couple of counterintuitive suggestions that can reduce the discomfort we typically feel right about now.

Our first suggestion is to *forgive your Friend* before you start. Forgive them? Aren't we here to apologize to them? And even though your Friend's forgiveness is absolutely not the point, and you have no right to expect it, deep down don't you hope they'll forgive you?

Yes, we're sure that would be wonderful. So why would we forgive them first? And how? And for what?

Be honest. You're uncomfortable, and isn't that at least partially their fault? Your relationship with your Friend is somewhat broken, and isn't *that* at least partially *their* fault? Even though you've done the work with your Fair Witness to know exactly what *you* did, isn't there even just a little bit of "what about *them*?" left for you?

That discomfort, that leftover blame and holding a grudge can leave you off-center, irritated, and defensive. And how you are *being*, when you meet with your Friend, will have a lot to do with the outcome of your apology.

What does it take to forgive someone? Perhaps it simply takes recognizing the other person's humanity, their frailty, their imperfection. In this way they're just like you—and us, sometimes doing or saying the wrong thing.

> We suggest that before you call your Friend, you find a way to forgive them in a private way, just to yourself, not out loud and certainly not to them.

Get present to their humanity and to yours. Aren't they just a person trying to get through the day, just like you? Forgive them just enough so that when you do talk to them, you aren't blaming them for the situation you both find yourselves in. Let them off the hook, so that when you do speak to your Friend, you're not a jerk. Seriously.

Once you have forgiven them (to yourself), it's time to approach your Friend.

Our second Step is this: Ask permission to apologize to them. Having to ask permission to apologize may seem counterintuitive. Why in the world would you need someone's permission to grovel to them? Because, if there is any chance of your apology being effective, it has to be their choice and their request to hear it.

You have forgiven your Friend just enough to get up the courage to approach them to make right what you have wronged. Now, imagine if you show up at their office or home with a bunch of flowers and a cheesy smile and they slam the door in your face. Let's avoid this scenario. Let's avoid it not least of all because one of the most shitty outcomes of any apology is the need to retreat and follow up with two apologies—one for the original "crime" and one for the first attempt at apologizing.

Asking permission to apologize is a crucial step that should be taken with great care. You are approaching someone with whom relations are strained or have been stuck. Your Friend may be surprised or even shocked to hear from you, so it's very important to put yourself in their shoes and understand how they might feel when hearing from you. While you can never really be so fully in their world that you can predict how they will react, doing your best to do so is an expression of friendship and compassion. **Never presume to know absolutely how they really feel.** At the end of the day, whatever your Friend's response is to your request has to be OK with you.

Frankly, giving your Friend the space and time to consider your request is the best way to accomplish this. You may be ready for a conversation, but your Friend may not. So, even if you contact them in person, rather than sending an email or text, or making a phone call, give them the chance to think about it and don't push for an immediate response.

Reach out to your Friend and say something like this: "I've been thinking about what happened between us and I feel bad. I'd like a chance to apologize to you properly. Can we get together, maybe have coffee?" You should keep clearly in mind that this meeting is for one reason only—for *you* to make *your* apology for what *you* have done and *nothing* else.

We've noticed that sometimes we might want to use this time to be forgiven, or to explain ourselves, or worse still to tell our Friend about all *their* mistakes. Please, please, please don't do this. It's a trap.

But . . . what in the world should you do if they say, "I don't want to meet later; why don't you just apologize now?" Be aware that this could happen. Every apology is different in some ways, and this response can feel like a kind of curveball, which may throw you off your game. The thing to remember is that the apology is for them, not you. So, if they are willing to hear you now instead of later, we suggest that you open your yap and give it your best shot.

We are giving you a kind of script—the Steps for apology. Have you ever seen a novice dancer trying to follow their newly learned steps for the Tango or whatever? More than likely, you will see someone who's not actually dancing. They may look clumsy and robotic, and they can quickly fall out of sync with the music and their partner.

At some point though, the Steps fade from their foreground while the music and their partner come alive for them. At this point they are truly dancing, fully present to the music and their partner. The Steps they originally learned are still there but in the background as a kind of muscle memory. It certainly keeps them upright, but they are no longer consciously counting steps or planning their next move. Consciously following dance steps isn't dancing.

Sometimes the steps of your apology will not be exactly as we wrote it or as you'd hoped for. Remember an apology is a conversation between two people; it's not a speech or lecture. Our best advice is, if you really want to make things right and if you want to have more freedom and happiness, be courageous and move forward. It's the practice of apologizing that makes you great at it.

We have yet to meet someone who is about to apologize who isn't at least a bit irritated, intimidated, or embarrassed by having to do it—even after all the previous work and private forgiveness. At this point, you don't have to be ready. You don't have to be serene.

You don't need to have everything you will say planned out and ready to go. You just need to contact them and ask them if you can apologize.

Make sure you read and understand the rest of these Steps before you do meet them.

Step Three: Say "I Am Really Sorry"

So, you know what you did, and you are ready to apologize. Actually . . . You're not quite ready. Having an understanding of what you've done and being willing to say "sorry" is great, and it's about as far as most people go when it comes to apologizing. The problem is, at this level of introspection the results are usually less than satisfying.

> **One reason our apologies can be weak is we tend not to acknowledge *how we were being* at the time of our transgression.**

Of course, every action we take, including speaking, comes along with the *Uninvited Guest* of our mood and our emotions. We're always feeling something! As just a few examples, are we generous, equitable, or stingy in how we behave with our Friends? We may not recognize those feelings because they are not always easy to see or to admit. Sometimes they are so consuming they have become like water to the fish.

No one *wants* to say, "I was being selfish," or childish, or greedy, or scared. Maybe it's easier to try to ignore our uninvited guests and hope they just leave of their own accord.

Guests in our lives can be good, bad, or indifferent, but we generally hope for some say in the matter! In any case, the kind of guest we're talking about here, nobody asked for, and they play both a part in the pickle we now find ourselves in and its solution.

Our actions and our uninvited guests are usually harmonious with each other in some way. For example, the act of giving to charity is often associated with generosity. But giving to charity could also come along with being self-aggrandizing. A person carrying a weapon could be a patriot or a criminal. The act of correcting a co-worker could be an expression of being supportive, but it can come hand in glove with being angry, impatient, or controlling.

BUT, if you blame what you did on your *uninvited guest*, you've actually stopped being responsible. You've become a victim of your own personality.

When John Lennon said in his song "I'm just a jealous guy," he was saying he had no control over himself. He was blaming his actions on his *uninvited guest* and in real life nobody wants to hear that, even though the song is really great. Presumably, he was *acting* poorly in some way to someone, *and* he was being jealous. That's what we're looking for here.

It doesn't matter in the least that you believe your uninvited guest led you to, or *made* you do what you did. If you express your apology in that way, you'll always look like you're not really sorry because you're not fully responsible. Don't do it.

So, your next task is to figure out how you were being when you did what you now know you did, and to include in your apology something along these lines: "I did X, I was being Y, I am so sorry."

We know we sound like a broken record, but in this formula there is no "because" linking the action with your uninvited guest. We never say we did X *because* we were being Y. This is crucial. For the listener, "because" always sounds like an excuse, something we are using to be let off the hook. The statement "I stole from you *because* I was jealous" could sound pathetic, and it is. "I stole from you. I was jealous, arrogant, thoughtless, and inconsiderate. I'm so sorry." . . . now you're talking. That little word "because" can sink your (relation)ship.

When it comes to admitting to the action itself and for the uninvited guest, straightforward, simple headlines are best. "I have been cold toward you." "I lied to you." "I stole your beer." It's not a soliloquy, or the great American novel. It's short and to the point.

Say, "I did X, I was being Y." Then, say "*I'm sorry.*"

Now, this is far from being a book about manners. The two grumpy old men who wrote it are nowhere near experts in etiquette. We may not use the right forks and spoons at dinner, but we're aware that for our interactions with others to go smoothly, certain words and phrases are essential. Put simply, phrases like please, thank you, excuse me, and sorry are the WD-40 of relationships. Use them.

Saying you are sorry won't heal the wound, but it might slow down the bleeding. People expect to hear it, and that's another important reason why it's a necessary part of the process.

Coolio Cools Out

Here is a quote from Coolio, the musician, when asked by journalist Dan Ozzi if he had gotten over an argument he was having with the musical satirist Weird Al Yankovic:

> I let that go so long ago. Let me say this: I apologized to Weird Al a long time ago and I was wrong . . . I took offense to [*Al's parody of Coolio*] . . . I was *being* cocky and shit and being stupid and I was wrong and I should've embraced that shit and went with it. [Emphasis added by the authors.]

This is great! In his own words, without excuses, he said, "I did X, I was being Y."

In Step Three, pay attention to this:

You are not looking for an excuse or a reason, so *never* include the word "because."

Be as sorry as you can be without being creepy. Don't try to prove how sincere you are. No crocodile tears. Be authentic.

This is about *your* actions, what you did, and how you did it, not at all about the other person's behavior. This isn't *Seinfeld*'s fake holiday Festivus—it's not a time to air your grievances or show feats of strength. **You can't ever, ever say what *they* did**. You can't say "I was an ass, but so were you," or "I wouldn't have stolen your money if you hadn't left it on the counter."

Don't ask for anything—especially not forgiveness or pity. There's no attack and no defense in an effective apology.

Step Four: Admit the Impact of Your Mistake

The word *admit* is very interesting, especially in the context of making an apology with the purpose of more freedom and more happiness. In the everyday use of the word, in the context of apology, according to the Oxford English Dictionary, admit means, "to confess to be true or to be the case." (I admit it! I stole your ice cream.) Clearly we want the person to whom we're apologizing to hear a truthful account of our actions.

But *admit* is also defined as to "allow in." Think of buying a ticket to a show or a sports event—your *admission* fee lets you into the venue. We usually think of our admission of the truth as being an outward action—we admit something to someone else. But in reality, our first admission is to ourselves. We let the truth in—we "allow" it in, in order to own it.

We suggest that it is impossible to fully admit your wrongdoings to another if you haven't admitted them to yourself.

What was the impact of our actions on our Friend? How do we find out and what does it look like when we truly admit it? It's not brain surgery. We begin by imagining. We put ourselves in their shoes.

This Step may take some planning. You're looking for ways that your actions have caused real-life consequences that led to your Friend's bad feelings. This is not always simple; in fact it goes without saying that you're not a mind reader. We are often blind to the ways our actions hurt people or sometimes it's just too hard to admit, or let in. And that doesn't even take into account the possible ripple effects of your actions—how they possibly also affected people other than your Friend. We strongly suggest that you talk to your Fair Witness to help you shed light on this.

When you speak to your Friend, tell them you have been thinking about how your actions may have affected them.

> **Say something like this . . . "I can't know for sure, but I can imagine that the way I behaved made you angry." Or "I've been cold and dismissive of your feelings. You've every right to be upset."**

These are just examples; you have to use your own words and tailor them to your specific situation. Be yourself—your Friend will know if you are not being genuine.

An Apology Is Not A Monologue, It's A Conversation.

After you have expressed how your actions may have made your Friend feel, now is the time to ask them the first of two essential questions. "Is that how it was for *you*? If you'd like to tell me, I'd really like to know."

It's possible that you nailed it when you told them how you thought your actions affected them. If you didn't, now you know and now you can own what you caused.

This may cause you some discomfort—you may cringe, but it's worth it. The healing process truly deepens if your Friend knows you have gone out of your way to put yourself in their shoes, to be in their world.

A word about how YOU might listen to what they have to say in response to Question #1: Don't resist it or deny it, don't justify it or explain it, and certainly don't defend it. You can't argue with them. They're telling you what happened to them and how *they* feel or felt—they're never wrong about that. Just let them know you actually heard what they said and that it matters to you. Once again, say sorry. Why not?

Now here's the second question. Ask them: "Is there anything more *you* want to say? Is there anything else I should know about?"

Brace yourself—whatever they say won't kill you, but it may sting. Repeat back what is said so that your Friend knows you've heard them. Show empathy and remorse for each detail as it comes. You may have an opinion about what they say, but your opinion is not the point. Whatever they say in response is the truth. Own it. After all, that's what you're there for.

Step Five: Promise You Can Be Trusted In the Future

By this time, you have truly listened to your Friend and you really know how your behavior affected them. If your Friend knows that your apology was authentic, you will notice some magic is beginning to happen. Of course, magic is an elusive thing to describe.

Perhaps you've seen examples of beautiful Japanese bowls with jagged lines of radiant gold running through them. These bowls didn't start out that way, but over time, through use and even carelessness, they broke. A skilled craftsman fixed the bowl using gold to stick the pieces together. The craftsman wasn't interested in repairing the bowl to hide the breakage but rather in using the gold to clearly show the places where the bowl was now fixed, making it stronger, more valuable, and even more beautiful than before.

This is Kintsugi, the Japanese art of precious scars.

This Japanese bowl is our analogy for the relationships in our lives where we've made a mistake, where there is a tear in the fabric or a crack in the clay that constitutes firm, satisfying, and working connections between ourselves and others. A broken bowl cannot hold anything that's poured into it and neither can a broken relationship. It doesn't matter how hard you try; if it's not fixed skillfully, it won't work.

The magic you are sensing as the result of all the hard work you've done so far is the potential of a stronger, more valuable, and even more beautiful relationship with your Friend. You are free from the reasons and explanations of yesterday and you are no longer trying to cover up your mistakes. Like the Kintsugi bowl, your imperfections can be golden scars you wear without regret.

> The next part of healing a broken relationship, of creating golden scars is by making a promise, a promise that you can be trusted in the future.

So the questions to ask yourself are: What should I be trustworthy about going forward? What do I need to commit to? What promise can I realistically make?

Here are some examples, but obviously you aren't limited to them. They are your promises to make.

- "I will not raise my voice to you in future."
- "In the future, I'll make sure I discuss important matters with you before acting."
- "I promise to trust you."
- "I promise to be more respectful."
- "I promise to be on time in the future—I'll make sure that I have an alarm on my phone that will give me plenty of time to get there."

Keep them short and on point, and make sure your Friend clearly understands what it is you're promising. Be very sure that whatever it is that you're promising is something you can commit to unreservedly. Try not to say you'll "try." It sounds non-committal. You could say "I'll be careful about. . . ."

Don't ever promise something you plan to figure out later. Never make promises you don't really mean (or that you don't think are important) just to look good or to slide on by.

If you look at our last example of being on time, you can see it really works to figure out in advance how you are going to keep that promise you made. In this case, we committed to setting an alarm.

So, how *are* you going to get the cash you promised to repay? How *are* you going to stop yourself from shouting? Before you make your promise, it's very valuable to consider practical strategies to *actually keep* your promise. Again, this would be a good discussion to have with your Fair Witness. You don't have to share this information with the person to whom you're apologizing; they don't need to know how the sausage is made, but it's well worth knowing it for yourself.

OK. Let's get real about promises. **A promise is not a guarantee**—you can't guarantee that you'll never make a mistake again, or even that you'll never *repeat* a mistake. For example, the odds of never being late again are slim. You give yourself half an hour to get to a meeting that's five minutes away and there's an unexpected forty-minute traffic jam. Shit inevitably happens.

The real question underneath your promise is how will you handle it if you *do* make that mistake again? How quickly will you own it and figure out how to do things better next time? How promptly will you let your Friend know that *you know* you broke your word and you are still committed to being on time?

There is beauty and power for yourself and your Friend in demonstrating that you are a person of your word—credible and serious. When you can't, for whatever reason, do as you promised, letting your friend know promptly shows you give a damn. It shows you are a person whose word means something and that the feelings of others matter to you.

So, where is the beauty and the power in this? **Being trustworthy changes who you are *for yourself*.** If you are dead serious about your promises and your commitments of all kinds, you undoubtedly become a new person. The more you practice being trustworthy, the more trustworthy you become for yourself. Your confidence grows and what's more, your friends, relatives, and coworkers know it and benefit from it, which in turn gives you more of the same. It's a feedback loop! The practice of being trustworthy is a guaranteed path to confidence and self-esteem.

Being late is a common mistake that everyone can understand. The costs involved on both sides are clear. Our claim is that even with much graver mistakes, the principle is the same. Certainly, there are no guarantees in life. If you have ever been untruthful in your life, how can you *guarantee* that it won't happen again? You can promise, and you should, but you can't ever guarantee. Even companies that provide actual written lifetime guarantees with their products can go bankrupt and leave you hanging. Solemnly signed contracts are broken all the time.

All the same: just make sure you don't ever use the old "a promise isn't a guarantee" as an excuse or justification for making a promise you don't intend to keep. A promise is a serious matter. It may not be a guarantee, but it is a serious commitment to change your behavior, to act differently.

In our example of a promise of honesty, you'd be giving your word to either be honest, and to admit you haven't been honest as soon as you can see your mistake. You'd clean up your broken promise and re-commit to it. That demonstrates *you* value your word. You then become valuable in your Friend's eyes. You become trustworthy, and being trustworthy brings freedom and happiness along with it. We promise!

A word about value. Although a promise is not a guarantee, that doesn't mean it is not precious. In fact, a promise adds real value to your relationship. Promises are not to be scattered around like birdseed. If you make a promise and break it, of course you can re-commit and promise again, but every time you make a promise without keeping it, your word becomes less valuable, and so do you. How many times have you heard, "I'll quit smoking tomorrow, I promise"? How cheap does it sound and just how trustworthy is the person who's saying it?

Step Six: Ask If You Can Do Anything More

Now is the time to ask your Friend, "Is there anything else I can do to make this right with you?"

So far you've asked them questions about how your behavior affected them, and you've based your promises on their responses. This final question allows your Friend to make any request of you that they wish.

Of course, you are free to say yes or no to their requests.

Why? Because now something is different. Now you are free! You are free because you are no longer blaming your Friend or yourself for your actions or your feelings.

You saw yourself as responsible for making your relationship work, and you now get to write the next chapter in the story of your Friendship. You have *ownership* of your own life, at least where this relationship is concerned. The simple fact is, the more relationships you heal, the more ownership you have of your life.

But not all of us are ready to take ownership of our lives. In fact, we could say: *don't* apologize if you are unwilling to give up being a victim in your life. Regaining your freedom and happiness in a broken relationship includes giving up the reasons and explanations you carry around. It means saying "I have something to do with the way things are in my life; I have something to do with the way I *experience* life." If you're not there, it's impossible to have the ownership we speak of.

If you make a mistake and apologize for it fully, but then your Friend requests that you make amends by coming over to paint their bathroom, you have the right to say "no, I can't commit to that"; unless, of course, your mistake was burning their house down, in which case, you'd be getting off lightly. Grab a brush.

Again, take your time. You're not obliged to make any rash decisions. Now you have the freedom to get back to them later with an answer. Just let them know when they can expect to hear from you.

Look: your Friend may not have a request prepared for you right away, but that doesn't mean they won't have one later. This isn't your Friend's last chance—always leave the door open for them to contact you and talk further.

Finally, say "thank you."

The freedom and satisfaction you are experiencing came directly from their generosity. You couldn't have done it without them.

Step Six and a Half: Don't Push It

At points throughout the process you will notice yourself feeling very different from when you began. When a relationship is broken, we often feel nervous, embarrassed, irritated, or even angry. Whatever the exact feeling, it was very likely to have been self-centered and defensive—our feelings and thoughts were centered on ourselves.

Now, at the end of Step Six, with nothing left to defend, we feel grateful to our Friend for the opportunity of freedom and of happiness. Our thoughts and feelings now include someone else. It's like an out-of-body experience! This is what people mean by a state of grace. It feels light and with less gravity. Less friction.

Maybe that's all a little too Magical Mystery Tour, but at the very least you'll be relieved. You'll be relieved that your Friend hasn't called for security or started yelling at you, or worse. And after all, you did what you came to do: you apologized. That took some doing, didn't it? And you probably did a pretty damn good job of it. So, you may feel a sense of satisfaction; you may feel relaxed and even a little giddy. You may by now be wondering why you took so long to apologize. That's how well this can work, but beware . . .

. . . your Friend may need a minute, a day, a week, or a decade to really believe that you are sincere and trustworthy. They are going through their own process of healing. They may think you are just trying to relieve your own guilt or simply get off the hook. They may find it tough to believe that you really will do what you said you would do. They may be wondering if it's even worth having a relationship with you at all. None of that is your concern.

You came to take ownership of your actions, and you did that. You did your best to put yourself in their shoes, imagining how your actions affected them. Now, stay there, in their shoes, by treating the process *they* are going through with respect. Give them the time and space they need to decide for themselves if they will forgive you.

Don't push it—and perhaps save your victory lap till you get home.

Part Two: Living the Steps

JASON'S FIRST ATTEMPT (AT APOLOGIZING)

"For the things we have to learn before we can do them, we learn by doing them."

—Aristotle, *The Nicomachean Ethics*

"Sucking at something is the first step toward being sorta good at something."

—Jake the Dog, *Adventure Time*

In the 1990s, I was living a less-than-healthy life in Manchester, UK. I was doing a lot of drugs and spending a lot of time watching TV and eating potato chips. This is hardly an unusual lifestyle for a young musician, but I did have certain responsibilities. The house I was living in belonged to my cousins, and they had graciously rented it to me knowing that I was not the most reliable of people. The tiny townhouse had two bedrooms, and in order to be able to afford the rent I needed a roommate. A friend of mine, Dave (not his real name), had recently lost his job, his girlfriend, and his apartment. We were kindred spirits. I knew Dave was looking for somewhere to stay, so I called him and within a few days he had moved in.

So, I am stoned, Dave is very drunk, and with the number of cigarettes and joints we were smoking, it's a wonder we didn't burn the house down. It's November in Manchester—wet and freezing cold and it gets dark at 4:00 p.m. We have no credit, and without credit the electricity company won't bill us every month. The company put a pay-meter in the house, and we had to put fifty English Pence in it to get the electricity working for a while. The power would constantly be going out, and when that happened we'd have to go out to find the money to turn on the TV, the heating, and everything else. We would get a couple of hours of heat and light and then . . . blackout. Of course, it was much more expensive than just receiving bills, but this was the situation we found ourselves in. Broke, cold, and unable to read a book in the evenings. As you can imagine, it was pathetic.

For me, however, there was quite literally a light (and heat!) at the end of the tunnel. My father lived in California, and I had a trip planned to visit him. Dad was paying for the trip, of course, although I was thirty-five years old, so off I flew to the Golden State, 65 degrees in

November, leaving Dave freezing in the dark.

At some point during my escape to California I got a call from Dave: "Jason, something terrible has happened: we've been robbed. Someone came into the house while I was in the shower, and they stole a bunch of your CDs and your leather biker jacket."

Now, I'm a drug addict—I'm not an idiot. It did dawn on me that none of his belongings were gone. I didn't believe Dave for a moment, but I couldn't prove that he was not being truthful.

I returned to the UK and to our den of iniquity. It's all a bit of a blur to me now, but I'm sure there was a new awkwardness between us. *In my mind*, I had decided that Dave had stolen from me and because of this, I could not trust him. Also, I didn't talk to him or anyone about my suspicions or the way I felt, and so my mistrust festered.

Not long after this, my cousins, who had been so generous and had risked so much by giving a drug addict the keys to their house—a real act of love and support—discovered that I was not sober. I had been lying to them. We had a big row, and they rightly threw me out of their house. It's called "tough love." That's another story, but of course Dave had to go too. I moved to the US, and I didn't speak to Dave again for a long time. Our relationship was broken.

Years later, having sobered up and having become convinced that my broken relationships were robbing me of my freedom and my happiness, I recounted this story to a trusted friend. I wanted to contact Dave and make an apology—I knew this was the key to making things right, but as far as I was concerned all that had happened was that I had given shelter to a man in need, and he had stolen from me. I couldn't figure out what I would be apologizing for! But knowing that I wasn't responsible for Dave's life, I had to look at the story again to try to discover my part in the breakdown of our relationship.

So, with the help of my Fair Witness, I looked at the story again. Back then, when I was living in my cousin's house, I needed a roommate. A decent person who cared about his cousins, their house, their income, and their peace of mind may have placed an ad in the local paper to look for a good, responsible person to share the house and the rent. I was none of the above, of course, and was really looking for someone who would ignore my lifestyle and allow me to carry on destroying myself and my relationship with my family. Good old Dave, down on his luck, and in the throes of alcoholism, fit the bill perfectly. Then, to add injury to insult I jetted off to the sunny shores of California leaving my "friend" to fend for himself in the cold and dark of Manchester in winter.

Dave is a great guy. It's important that you know this—when he's not drinking he's one of the best. But in this situation what was he supposed to do? I suspected that he had stolen a few CDs and a leather jacket, sold them to some consignment place, and used the money to heat the house, keep a light on, and God forbid, buy a couple of cans of beer. Suddenly I could see I had set my Friend up to fail. The loss of a couple dozen CDs and a jacket looked meaningless in comparison to the underhanded way I had behaved.

This discovery left me gob smacked. I felt completely humiliated. I was shocked to realize the harm I had done, selfishly using a supposed friend as cover for my crappy behavior and lifestyle. Since this had happened I had owned hundreds of CDs and I replaced all the music that had been stolen. Dozens of jackets had come and gone to the thrift store, but my relationship with Dave seemed unfixable. Frankly I was quite disgusted with myself.

Five years had gone by since this had all happened, and it took a little doing but I found an email address for Dave and asked him to call me, which he did. He said he was really shocked to hear from me. Almost immediately he admitted he'd stolen my belongings and began apologizing. I let him talk and then quietly began a heartfelt apology of my own. I stated what I had done and asked him if I had forgotten anything. I asked how it all had affected him. I told him I was so, so sorry for the wasted years when we could have been friends, and I promised him I'd be a better friend in the future (and I have been). I let him know I had no bad feelings and I didn't care about the CDs—I cared about him. I asked him if there was anything I could do to help him feel better about the whole thing. In my own clumsy way, I was hoping to restore Dave's happiness and sense of wellbeing as well as my own.

Years have passed and while we live a half world away from each other, the only thing that there is between us now is our friendship. We are both free from the past.

By the way, my cousins and I couldn't be closer. I made my apology and expressed my deep regret for what I did—and once a year I call to say that I haven't forgotten about this. I am so grateful to them for the home, the trust, and for throwing me out!

I DECIDED YOU WERE WRONG

"Out beyond ideas of wrongdoing and rightdoing there is a field. I'll meet you there."

—Rumi

"If you spit in the air, it lands on your face."

—Yiddish proverb

In Jason's anecdote, perhaps you can begin to see the incredible power of apology to tear down the walls we have built around ourselves. The walls that we thought were protecting us were, in fact, keeping us imprisoned. As time goes by, we increase the number of people we'd prefer to avoid (or boil in a vat of acid) and we decrease the size of our community, one person at a time, like shooting cans off a shelf at a fairground. As we shut people off, any opportunity or possibility that the relationship may have presented, no matter how seemingly insignificant, or unclear, or unknown, is lost.

Many times, we have been asked something like, "how do I use apology to fix my relationship with so-and-so when I have searched the corners of my soul and can't find anything to apologize for?" So-and-so is simply, well, a jerk.

Sometimes it's truly difficult to find something tangible to apologize for.

Here's an example. There's a cast of characters whose names we've changed to protect their confidentiality.

Simon: our Friend
Daisy: Simon's mom
Henry: Simon's stepfather

Simon's parents split up when he was very young. Both his mother and his father remarried a few years later and started second families. Simon was fortunate to have a great relationship with his dad, his dad's new wife, and the new wife's kids.

Simon's mom Daisy, on the other hand, could be difficult. Simon says she was moody and self-centered, a hypochondriac, and not a lot of fun to be around. Additionally, her new husband Henry, according to Simon, was an opinionated and unlikable man, and rather controlling, especially where Daisy was concerned. Henry's children, who were still at home, seemed to come first in every regard.

Simon moved to a different city, but when he was in town, he visited his mother, mostly out of a sense of duty. When Simon would invite Daisy for coffee or a walk for some alone time together, his mom would always find an excuse to say no.

Simon suspected that his mother was nervous about what her husband would say if she did want time alone with her son. It seemed to Simon that Henry was jealous of Simon's love for his mother. Each time Simon asked to see his mom, he suffered the pain of rejection only a child can feel, and he blamed Henry.

For decades, Simon loathed Henry. He hated his political opinions, his notions about religion, and his impatience with Daisy. The sound of Henry's voice began to drive Simon nuts; he hated the way Henry sniffed arrogantly when he ended a sentence or how Henry rolled his eyes with disdain when he disagreed with something. Underlying all these seemingly petty crimes, Simon blamed Henry for taking away the possibility of any closeness with his mother.

Of course, Simon never expressed these feelings to Henry or to his mom. After all, they were adults, and he didn't live with them. Their relationship was none of his business and he didn't want to rock the boat. At least his mom was taken care of, and Simon was able to see her when he was home, albeit with a chaperone!

Simon is an expert apologizer, but this situation had flummoxed him for years. He knew his relationship with Henry was a hot mess, but how would an apology fix it? Apologize for what? For wanting to spend time with his mother? Simon sincerely couldn't find anything to apologize for.

We encouraged Simon to step out of his head for a moment, away from his suppositions and the probabilities about how his mom felt or what she thought—away from his opinions about Henry's personality and his motivations, and away from his own anxieties and yearning for his mother's love.

We asked Simon to consider, for a moment, that his mother's husband, for all his human failings, loved Daisy. He certainly loved her enough to keep a roof over her head and ensure her safety. Daisy wasn't the easiest of people—her hypochondria resulted in countless trips to the hospital that turned out to be false alarms. Henry had stuck with her through thick and thin. Sure, Henry was a jerk at times, but hey, who isn't? And anyway, jerkish-ness is in the eye of the beholder and Simon didn't live with Henry, so why did he care? Henry wasn't wrong.

***Henry wasn't wrong*. Let that sink in for a moment. Henry had been infected with "wrongness," like he might have caught a virus. And who had infected Henry with the wrongness? Simon.**

Henry *was* wrong, just not in the physical world. Henry was wrong in Simon's head! Simon had *decided* Henry was wrong! He had looked at all the circumstances of Daisy and Henry's relationship, and his conclusion? Henry was wrong.

Had Daisy decided that Henry was wrong? No, in fact she loved him, was thankful for him and wanted to spend her life with him. Simon's problem wasn't Henry. Simon's problem was his own decision about Henry. To Simon's credit, once he looked at it from this new angle, he discovered what part he had played in his relationship with Henry and Daisy.

Simon had infected Henry with The Wrongness, and only Simon had the antidote.

So, Simon picked up the phone and said something like the following: "Hi Henry, it's Simon. Do you have a minute? I'm calling because I've been thinking about you and how great you've been for my mom. I'm so grateful to you for looking after her. I know that it's not always easy. I also want to apologize to you. I know we haven't always seen eye-to-eye and we've had some arguments, especially about politics and religion, and I've come to realize how easily I can get irritated over stuff that's not really very important. I'm so sorry: I had decided you were wrong, and you are not wrong. Far from it—you have loved my mom and raised a family you can be proud of. That's what's important. That's what's real. I'm sure you have felt my anger, and I think it hurt you and I want you to know I'm sorry."

Simon went on to ask the questions we recommend in this book and promised to be different going forward.

The next time Simon visited Henry and Daisy, he plucked up the courage to suggest a walk in the local park, just him and his mom. To his enormous surprise, before Daisy could answer, Henry said, "Go on love, why don't you? I'll put the kettle on for when you get back."

This is what freedom and happiness looks like.

On reflection, there is an even more important lesson in Simon and Henry's story than simply how to apologize well. By putting Henry in a box so early on in their relationship, Simon shaped both his own and Henry's behavior. Simon's demeanor toward Henry had always been defensive and passive-aggressive. How could it have been otherwise when Henry was from the beginning pegged as "wrong"? And of course, it meant that Henry didn't really care for Simon.

Additionally, by deciding Henry was wrong, Simon had also inadvertently cast his mom as Henry's victim. He had determined that his mother wasn't even allowed to take a short walk alone with her son. In the world that Simon had created in his head, everything reinforced his decision that Henry was a bully and that included his mother having to *be* bullied. Without realizing it, Simon had turned his mother into a very small person. And of course, Simon couldn't speak up. After all, everyone knew that Henry was a bully, and Daisy wasn't strong enough to handle confrontation.

In the world that Simon had created, there was no way for Simon to relate to Henry and Daisy as family. And there is no doubt that Henry and Daisy acted toward Simon accordingly, leaving Simon even more isolated and certain of his perspective.

From this perspective you can clearly see that Simon wasn't the victim as he first thought, but rather he was a major player in the entire family dynamic.

So, without this revelation, what would this family's life have looked like? As Shakespeare said:

> Tomorrow, and tomorrow, and tomorrow,
> Creeps in this petty pace from day to day,
> To the last syllable of recorded time

In short: If nothing changes, nothing changes.

The Wrongness

Everyone has experienced the lingering sensation that something about us is wrong. Wrong job, wrong parents, wrong partner, wrong background, wrong education, wrong looks, etc., etc., ad infinitum. A friend of ours who has sponsored hundreds of people in a 12-Step group likes to say, "Breasts come in two sizes, too big and too small. Penises come in one size—too small." We're all walking around thinking something's wrong most of the time: I'm late, I'm early, I'm lost, I never, I'm always, I could, I should, and on and on.

In each of these examples, nothing is really, factually wrong. In each case, wrongness is assigned by us and is merely our interpretation. We have injected ourselves with The Wrongness, and only we have the antidote.

Let's use our favorite example of "being." Have you ever been late? I bet you have, and sometimes you thought you were wrong for being late, and other times you felt completely justified. The lateness was the same, you were late. What was the difference? Your perception of the incident.

Imagine how you would feel if someone who has been difficult to you in your life, looked you in the eye and sincerely said, "You are not wrong, I *decided you were wrong*, and I'm sorry."

To hear "you are not wrong" is an enormous relief. Sometimes it's what you've been waiting to hear all your life.

And what if all the wrongness you assigned *yourself* melted away? What if you just weighed what you weighed, not too much or too little? What if *you* became all right with *yourself*?

APOLOGIES IN A MINOR KEY

"A life spent making mistakes is not only more honorable, but more useful than a life spent doing nothing."

—George Bernard Shaw

"Apologize when you're wrong instead of find quotes to support your stupidity."

—Anonymous

For those who love old movies, it's hard to forget the famous tagline of *Love Story*: "Love Means Never Having to Say You're Sorry." On the other hand, John Lennon said "Love means having to say you're sorry every 15 minutes." We're not sure which is truer, but we, the authors of *The Glory of Groveling*, notice that we hear the word "sorry" every day, either from ourselves or the people we deal with on a daily basis. Sometimes more than one per day.

"Sorry, I'm late." "Sorry I interrupted you." "Sorry I bumped into you." "Sorry, I wasn't listening." "Sorry, not sorry."

And if we don't say sorry, we say something like it.

So what's going on here? These examples are clearly not the planned and thoughtful apologies we've been discussing in the previous chapters. **However, these small apologies are the oil that keeps the wheels of our relationships turning.**

An Old Joke by an Anonymous Comedian

A man walks into a bar, sits down, and orders a drink. The bartender hands him his drink, accompanied by a bowl of peanuts.

To the man's surprise, a voice comes from the peanut bowl. "You look great tonight!" it said. "So handsome. . . And that aftershave is just wonderful!"

The man is obviously a little confused by the voice but tries to ignore it.

Realizing he has no cigarettes; the man wanders over to the cigarette machine. After he inserts his money, the

machine says, "You ugly BASTARD. . . see a doctor, you stink and your face looks like a donkey's dinner."

By now, the man is extremely perplexed. He turns to the bartender for an explanation.

"Ah, yes sir," the bartender responds, "The peanuts are complimentary, but the cigarette machine is out of order."

Funny? Not funny? Never mind: What's the point?

You and I are often "out of order" when we're being some way or doing something that is inconsistent with our values, or the way we'd like to live our lives. And we know it.

On any average day, we, the writers of this book, have been known to be guilty of at least one of the following:

Being thoughtless
Being rude
Not listening
Being angry
Being self-centered
Ignoring the feelings of other people
Being impatient
Being demanding
Being humorless
Being negative
Being judgmental
Prejudging someone
Being uncaring
Not being compassionate
Being closed-minded
Being forceful or coercive

Being less than serious
Being too serious
Being untruthful
Being lazy
Being arrogant
Being impudent
Being disrespectful
Being flip
Being childish
Being discourteous
Being sneaky
Being catty
Being derogatory
Being unkind
Being inconsiderate
Being insensitive
Being self-absorbed
Being dismissive

The list can go on forever, and we are not psychopaths (we've been tested) and you too are unlikely to be one. Of course, these are not federal offenses, but anyone can see how any one of these transgressions can cause problems between people.

What we're getting at here is that there are, to use legal terms, misdemeanors and there are felonies. Our everyday misdemeanors—an inappropriate word or phrase, a spilled drink, an elbow on the subway—are easily fixed with the small fine payable as a minor apology.

If these misdemeanors remain unacknowledged and disowned and they increase in

number, they can accumulate in the *world of the offended person* and become felonies remarkably fast.

Imagine if a coworker accidentally stepped on your toes every lunchtime and never said anything about it. The first time they did it you may let it go, but half a dozen times later you'd be banging on the door of HR, if not the sheriff's office.

Or, depending on your position or your disposition, you may explode, or you may simply take your marbles and go home. It's happened to all of us. Seemingly out of nowhere, we, or someone else just blows up. We've all heard the expression or even said it . . . "it got so bad, I finally had to do something." Those are the moments when all the misdemeanors add up to one big crime, and we now see our Friend as a felon who is out to do us wrong.

Voices are raised, emotions run high, and everything starts seeming very dramatic. Whether you are attacking or defending, at the very least there's an unpleasant break in the flow of life for all concerned.

In cases like these, someone has been on the receiving end of hurtful behavior or words, and resentment has slowly built up. Often, neither party fully realizes the rising tension—so when things finally explode, it can come as a shock to both.

How many times have you been surprised by the level of someone's reaction? We say things like, "I really didn't know you felt that way," or "I didn't know you had been holding on to that." Or, how many times have we been surprised at our own great big reaction to something small?

It all begins with something light, maybe just a barely noticeable pebble in our shoe. But because these misdemeanors were never resolved, the pebbles kept adding up until the discomfort became too great to not react.

How do we deal with this phenomenon? How do we choose to lose the blues caused by the pebble in our shoe?

Just as there are varying degrees of misdeed in life, there are also different levels of apology. There are as many opinions about this as there are people who've thought about it. We suggest, however, that there are actually only two types worth considering. The first is the one we've been discussing and describing in this book up until now (and suggesting a solution for). The other is this: The Minor Apology.

Although these apologies are different in scale, in essence they are the same. They are both designed to provide freedom and happiness for all parties in a relationship through an honest ownership of our actions and attitude.

Notice we haven't referred to an *honest expression* of feelings. Remember when restoring a broken relationship, your feelings are inconsequential to your Friend. It is *our* ownership of our actions (including our words) and *how we were being* that allows for freedom and happiness. In fact, our experience overwhelmingly tells us that when we are *honest* about these things, *our* feelings improve.

For the minor apology, speed is of the essence. The healing we will create is proportional to the speed of recognizing and apologizing for our misdemeanor.

So how do you know when a minor apology is required?

Pay attention to two things: the impact you are having on your environment—the people with whom you're interacting—and your own sense of freedom and happiness. Are you feeling uncomfortable?

This sense of something being wrong *somewhere* can appear at the time of the offense or later, when reviewing an interaction, but again, the speed with which you acknowledge your shit and say sorry will be proportional to the healing that you will create.

In other words, the faster you acknowledge your mistakes and apologize authentically, the more healing you will create.

But more than that, each small apology is a chance to tidy the mess and relieve the stress that a mistake, a minor offense, or a clumsy remark or action can cause between people.

Once again, if we don't take care of these infractions quickly and with integrity, the mess and the stress grow to the point of a much more serious breakdown.

Michael's Personal Example

Out to dinner with Friends recently I became irritated for no apparent reason. The company was great, the food was good, the service was excellent but no matter, I was annoyed with everyone and began treating my wife and friends as if they were the enemy. Honestly, I have no idea why. Maybe my back hurt, maybe I was tired, but I really didn't know. It's not like I was yelling and insulting everyone, but I began to be humorless, and then I started getting snarky, and finally I was annoyed with everyone and everything they said. All this happened very quickly, much faster than it took for you to read about it.

I knew something was up because of *my* level of discomfort. It made me realize I was not being or acting in a manner that anyone deserved or appreciated. I began to imagine what I would leave my friends and wife with if I didn't clean up my act. What would they later say about me after I had basically taken a big dump in the middle of our night together?

It took me an hour of being annoyed before I could see my annoyance was in no way caused by my friends, it was ALL me. I wish I could have seen it sooner, but I was grateful I saw it at all. I stopped being a jerk at once and I knew I needed to apologize for being "out of order."

Back in the car, before we drove home, I turned to my wife and friends and said "I owe everyone an apology. I was being annoying and acting like a jerk and I have no reason to be. I am really sorry for my behavior tonight."

The result was immediate and positive. One Friend said that they didn't notice anything, and no apology was needed. The other Friend was grateful; saying, "you are lovely! I was wondering if you were OK, and I appreciate the apology." My wife didn't say anything, just nodded and smiled. She knows me all too well. I'm a lucky guy.

The whole apology took no more than two minutes and what did I accomplish? I restored my own integrity. I owned my own crassness and stopped blaming everyone and everything else. I let my Friends know that I was aware of the negative effect I had on the evening and that it wasn't OK for me to do that. I prevented this small crack in our Friendship from ever having the chance of getting larger.

Jason's Personal Example

My angelic and incredibly patient wife, Ava, has a long and ever-expanding list of "Honey-do's." The list is so long that if I wait just a short while, even she will forget what was on it a while ago. That means that, in effect, I don't have to do very much. I am blessed.

Sometimes, though, she'll really need me to do something. Recently, one morning, I was leaving the apartment for my day job at our local radio station and, while I was gathering my stuff for the day—phone, laptop, coffee, headphones, keys, notes, sandwich, meds, etc., Ava asked me to swing by the pharmacy on my way home and pick something up.

I mumbled a cursory "Sure," or a "Yes Dear," or whatever, and stumbled, still half asleep, out the door. Of course, you guessed it, after work I drove straight home. Stumbling back through the door, I kicked off my shoes and lay down on the couch with Mrs. Pickles, our family dog.

Ava walked in and the conversation went something like this:

A: Did you go to the pharmacy for me?

J: What?

A: The pharmacy. I asked you this morning.

J: When this morning?

A: You were getting ready to go to work.

J: You asked me something important in my first hour awake? Before I'd had so much as a half a cup of coffee? How many times do I have to tell you . . .

You can imagine how this interaction became unpleasant very quickly. Ava rolled her eyes and left the room, the dog went under the table, and I was left on the couch, irritated, embarrassed, and alone.

Not only had I neglected to listen to Ava's earlier request, but I had also pretended to hear her by answering "sure." I had, in my usual self-centered way, gone through my day without recalling her needs or calling to ask if she needed anything; and when she asked if I'd remembered, I was defensive, impatient, humorless, impudent, disrespectful, childish, discourteous, inconsiderate, self-absorbed, and more, all in the space of ninety seconds.

In the morning, I neglected my wife. I was being selfish and not listening. And now I'd tried to blame her for my *thoughtlessness*. How embarrassing!

I went into the other room and apologized. I mentioned everything in the paragraph above. I didn't need an appointment, or a Fair Witness or a glass of Dutch courage. I needed to say sorry. Ava smiled and thanked me. She's very forgiving. I am, as I said, blessed.

Oh—and I put my shoes back on and took the dog for a walk to the pharmacy.

CRAPOLOGIES

That didn't happen.
And if it did, it wasn't that bad.
And if it was, that's not a big deal.
And if it is, that's not my fault.
And if it was, I didn't mean it.
And if I did, you deserved it

The Narcissist's Prayer—*Dayna Craig*

Sorry, but we're not sorry if you're offended by our lovely term, "Crapology" as a way of pointing out how shitty most apologies are. Most apologies just don't work, and by that we mean most apologies really don't deliver much in the way of freedom and happiness for either party. So, let's have a little fun and look at a selection of bad apologies that tickle our fancy as an opportunity to point out some of the more common mistakes people make while apologizing.

We've used the attempted apologies of celebrities and other famous people as our examples. We are not judging the behavior that preceded the apologies or even the character of the people who are making them. Honestly, we don't know what these folks actually did or didn't do that led to their apology. We only have their publicly published apologies to go on, and it is only those apologies that we are making fun of, in the sole interest of learning from them.

We should say, from the start of this chapter, that we, the writers, don't consider what are commonly called Public Apologies to be our kind of apologies at all. For the most part, they never seem to conform to our definitions of apology; in fact they usually look like something else altogether.

Since you have gotten this far in reading our thoughts and our process, we hope you'll have gotten the sense that we consider a well-made apology to be something very valuable indeed, usually made between two people, eye to eye, in which hearts are opened and vulnerabilities bared. In this way, they are often intimate, and the whole is greater than the sum of the parts. In other words, they're special.

A public apology, as we're about to see, is often just a way for people who have been publicly embarrassed or "found out," to keep their job and/or protect their income. Commonly, the public apology won't include the apologizer taking full responsibility for their deeds or making amends. They are typically filled with blame and justifications.

In many public apologies, there are at least two parties who are injured, the public in general and the people directly affected. For example, when Will Smith slapped Chris Rock at The Oscars on live TV, in front of millions, it's obvious that Chris was hurt and deserved an apology. No doubt the members of The Academy of Motion Picture Arts and Sciences were also affected along with the producers of the show. These types of actions deserve the kind of apologies we cover in this book, the kind of apologies that everyday people make every single day, where we actually have to ask our Friends how it was for them and how we can make it right. This is impossible to do with a public apology, and the public can smell the bullshit.

On the other hand, millions of us saw the "slap heard around the world" and we too were affected. Perhaps we were offended; maybe we had to explain it to our children. Maybe we decided we'd never watch another Will Smith movie. This is where the public apology comes in, as an attempt to lessen the damage to one's career.

There are so many really horrible, often funny and strangely interesting Crapologies online. Just Google "really horrible apologies" like we did, and you will find 34,500,000 entries in .53 seconds.

While we mean to have a bit of fun with these, knowing about these pitfalls can save a ton of time and heartache as you navigate your future free and happy life of apology.

Fame, by the way, in our limited experience, is no fun when people find out that you're human. It only adds to the burden.

A Recipe for Disaster

While our first Crapology may seem like something you would see on a Saturday Night Live skit, the following actually happened. In 2017, the restaurant news website *Eater* reported that four women had accused celebrity chef Mario Batali of sexual harassment and sexual assault.

Almost immediately, Batali responded twice publicly, first on CNN where he said, "I apologize to the people I have mistreated and hurt. That behavior was wrong and there are no excuses. I take full responsibility and am deeply sorry for any pain, humiliation, or discomfort I have caused to my peers, employees, customers, friends, and family."

Knowing what you know now about real apologies, it's easy to see how terrible and frankly insulting this apology is—but it gets so much worse . . .

Batali goes on to say, "We built these restaurants so that our guests could have fun and indulge, but I took that too far in my own behavior. I won't make that mistake again."

Batali followed up this apology a few days later in an online newsletter. He repeated himself almost word for word, only adding a generic promise to work to regain his readers' "respect and trust."

Then, directly after, above a large color photo of a very tempting sweet cake, Batali wrote, "P.S. In case you're searching for a holiday inspired breakfast, these pizza dough cinnamon rolls are a fan favorite."

Hard to believe, but it's not hard to find the actual newsletter on the internet.

PRACTICE SESSION: Aside from being terrible and insulting, in light of what we now know about the power of a well-made apology, this apology is clearly not designed to create freedom and happiness for anyone, least of all poor old Mario. There are *at least* three missed opportunities in Mario's apologies. Can you find and describe them? This is great practice. Remember, however, that the idea is not to judge Mario. We've all made mistakes, some more consequential than others. The point is to become familiar with effective apologies.

Here are three missed opportunities we came up with . . .

1. He didn't publicly apologize to the women for his actions.
2. He reduced the significance of what he was accused of.

3. He didn't publicly say what he could be counted on in the future.

P.S. Those pizza dough cinnamon rolls looked deadly.

Where's LaBeouf?

Here's another one that really tickled our funny bones, found in Graeme McMillan's article for *Wired* magazine on December 17, 2013, titled "Shia LaBeouf May Have Plagiarized His Apology for Plagiarism." *Are you kidding us?*

According to the article, Mr. LaBeouf first issued a series of Tweets apologizing for completely plagiarizing a graphic novel by renowned creator Daniel Clowes. Mr. LaBeouf was working on a movie at the time. The film was allegedly an almost exact copy of the graphic novel.

Shia LaBeouf's apologies were made as posts on what was then called Twitter. Perhaps this was his first mistake. Part of these apologetic "tweets" included a definition of the term "copying and creativity" that read suspiciously like one already posted by a user on Yahoo! Answers. No credit was given to the original author.

Here are his tweets . . .

"Copying isn't particularly creative work. Being inspired by someone else's idea to produce something new and different IS creative work."
—Shia LaBeouf (@thecampaignbook) December 17, 2013

"In my excitement and naiveté as an amateur filmmaker, I got lost in the creative process and neglected to follow proper accreditation."
—Shia LaBeouf (@thecampaignbook) December 17, 2013

"I'm embarrassed that I failed to credit @ Danielclowes for his original graphic novella 'Justin M. Damiano', which served as my inspiration."
—Shia LaBeouf (@thecampaignbook) December 17, 2013

"I was truly moved by his piece-of-work & I knew that it would make a poignant & relevant short. I apologize to all who assumed I wrote it."
—Shia LaBeouf (@thecampaignbook) December 17, 2013

"I deeply regret the manner in which these events have unfolded and want @Danielclowes to know that I have a great respect for his work."
—Shia LaBeouf (@thecampaignbook) December 17, 2013

"I fucked up."
—Shia LaBeouf (@thecampaignbook) December 17, 2013

So, what is there to learn from Shia's apology?

Public apologies are not really apologies at all.

Don't end with "I fucked up." Start with it.

Don't give *reasons* for your actions. Your reasons *always* sound like excuses to *everyone* else.

Some good questions to ask ourselves are: Why do we feel so obligated to give a reason or an explanation when we are apologizing? Why don't we simply say what we did, in clear, simple language and leave it at that? Why do we almost always want to provide "context" or "background" or to tell our story about how the whole thing looked to us? What are we hoping for? What do we get out of this strange knee-jerk behavior?

In LaBeouf's apology he says he got lost in the sauce. He was so excited and so inexperienced, he didn't give full credit to the original author. But Shia isn't alone. We all want to explain *why* we messed up.

Moreover, does that explanation really matter? What if he had said, I was left-handed and therefore I . . .? Or I did it because my father was bald . . .? Does either explanation actually change what Shia did or what he is apologizing for? Does either explanation change how Mr. LaBeouf will make amends to Mr. Clowes?

Presumably, LaBeouf thought so.

This is the thing: Apologizers always think that their story about what happened provides context and gives important reasons for what they did. Everyone else, on the other hand, always hears those reasons as excuses, i.e., bullshit. They always come across as what lawyers call "mitigation."

Mr. LaBeouf isn't unique in always having an explanation. It's part of our humanity. And this is what this part of our humanity is all about . . . Lessening the impact of our mistakes on *ourselves*. We seem to think that a good enough explanation will have us walking away with less to apologize for, less of a negative impact on our reputation, and less to pay for in our amends. We can keep our view of ourselves as a good person, who only made a mistake due to whatever our explanation is. In LaBeouf's explanation he was "excited and naive." This is designed, consciously or unconsciously, to allow his public and his employers to still see him as trustworthy, innocent and only human. You really can't fault that, can you?

Our explanations are a device to make us look good—to others and to ourselves.

What have we all done, in the name of looking good? We've pretended we've heard someone when we haven't. We pretend we've understood someone when we haven't. We looked to see who saw us when we tripped walking down the hall. We've told little white lies when our partners asked us how they looked. We've not raised our hands to answer the question, fearing we'd be wrong. We didn't volunteer to take on the next big job because we feared we would fail. We didn't speak up when someone gossiped about a friend. We've ordered a salad at lunch to avoid looking like a glutton. We've told people we just worked out when we actually spent an hour at the gym in the steam room. We stayed in an unworkable romantic relationship because we didn't want to be the "bad guy."

Pretense is at the heart of all of these things. Pretending that we are always good, sincere people when in fact, from time to time we lie, steal, and cheat. We desire to be admired, and we will mitigate the times when we are less than admirable.

People do these things to avoid facing the music. To avoid the truth about their lives. Unfortunately, the music of our lives is often out of tune! And, to mix our metaphors, these pretentious actions simply add to the "psychic weight" that we talked about in our first chapter and rob us of our freedom and happiness.

So, the problem is that the more we mitigate, the more we pretend, the less freedom and happiness we create. And it gets worse, because it's not a 50/50 deal.

A teacup of reasons, explanations, and mitigation loses us a swimming pool of freedom and happiness.

Why? Because we've relinquished the authority and power over our lives to our excuses, just to look good in the moment.

Your life either belongs to you or to your excuses.

Now, we know that the word "because" is an absolute red flag when it comes to apologizing in order to create freedom and happiness, but we should always check ourselves for *any* kind of mitigation. It is, put simply, just a way to look good in the face of our own shitty behavior.

However, if the person to whom you're apologizing asks you why you did something, you can always, as humbly as possible, tell them. Keep it short.

First-Class Crapology

In 2017, a United Airlines Kentucky-bound trip was overbooked. Four passengers were randomly selected to be bumped off the flight.

One of the four was Dr. David Dao, who had patients in a hospital in Kentucky. Dr Dao told the airline staff it was crucial that he examine the patients the next morning. Dao refused to comply with the demand to exit the plane and wouldn't leave.

In the smartphone age, unfortunately for United, a video shot by a fellow passenger was posted to the web showing Dao being forcibly dragged from his seat by security agents and removed violently from the plane. The video quickly went viral.

The apology from United's Chief Executive Oscar Munoz included the following statement: "This is an upsetting event to all of us here at United. I apologize for having to re-accommodate these customers. Our team is moving with a sense of urgency to work with the authorities and conduct our own detailed review of what happened."

Wow. This is really brilliant Crapology. You really couldn't make it worse, could you, unless you come out and say "We were glad to drag this dude off the plane. And, to those of you who saw this event with your own eyes on YouTube, you are unqualified to assess the truth of the situation. That will take our own investigation, the results of which will be the final word. So there."

Mr. Munoz used the word "re-accommodate" as a synonym for violently dragging a perfectly sober medical doctor who was concerned for his patients' well-being, by the arms, kicking and screaming from a packed airplane.

This is an example of what George Carlin called "Soft Language," and of what another famous George, Mr. Orwell, called "Doublethink."

Carlin says Soft Language is "language that takes the life out of life and makes things worse." Examples he gives include "you were not *fired*, you were *downsized*," "The government doesn't *lie*, it engages in *misinformation*," and "The Pentagon actually measures nuclear radiation in something they call *Sunshine Units*!" The emphasis is ours!

Using this kind of language instead of being clear about what you did in a straightforward way, abdicates you from responsibility and makes the listener doubt your honesty.

Step Two of the Six and a Half Steps of Groveling, urges you to "take out the explanations, the whys, the because-s, the feelings, the what-*they*-did, and just focus on *what you did* or *did not do.*"

Step Three relates: "When it comes to admitting to the action itself and how you were feeling, straightforward, simple headlines are best. 'I have been cold toward you.' 'I lied to you.' 'I stole your beer.' It's not a soliloquy, or the great American novel. It's short and pointed. Say, 'I did X, I was being Y.' Then, say '*I'm sorry*.'"

Clearly, United didn't say "We manhandled Dr. Dao forcibly off of a flight which we knew was important to him and his patients, because we had overbooked the seats. We're sorry." That would be a great start and of course, there are a number of other steps to righting this wrong.

Finally, notice that Mr. Munoz expressed, "This is an upsetting event to all of us here at United." *Ahhh, we feel so terribly for the poor guy, and his upset organization!* An important point in the Six and a Half Steps of Groveling is that the pathway to freedom and happiness takes the focus off of you. Put your feelings in the background and focus on the person you are apologizing to. It is OK to have the feelings you have, but take the significance out of them. Don't make your feelings more important than your Friend, at least while apologizing.

We know that this is no simple task, especially when you are inexperienced in the practice of placing your feelings in the background and doing what works—the Six and a Half Steps.

Think back to your first attempt at riding a bike—how many times did you fall? How hard was it to make even a few yards? Yet, after trying time and time again, you developed muscle memory and balance and were able to ride forever.

Our mantra for all this is "Get over yourself!" Now, make it yours.

A Fuzzy Apology

In April of 1997, the *New York Times* reported that Fuzzy Zoeller, a very successful professional golfer, had insulted Tiger Woods, one of the most famous American sportsmen of all time.

The article stated: "In a taped interview that was shown on CNN, Zoeller called Woods a 'little boy' and urged him not to request fried chicken and collard greens at next year's Champions Dinner at the Augusta National (Golf) Club. In an initial apology on Monday, and again yesterday, Zoeller said he was joking. Zoeller said, "It's too bad that something I said in jest was turned into something it's not, but I didn't mean anything by it and I'm sorry if I offended anybody. If Tiger is offended by it, I apologize to him, too."

This is what experts call the "Non-apology apology." Comedian Harry Shearer has coined the term "If-pology" on "The Apologies of the Week" segment of his syndicated radio program, *Le Show*.

We like to label it the "If-Then Crapology," because the label tells you what's in the can. We've all done this, it's very common, seemingly innocent and sincere, but it is deceptive and incredibly destructive.

The If-Then Crapology denies responsibility. It takes you out of the shoes of the person to whom you're apologizing. These are the very shoes we say are necessary to step into for a true understanding of the damage you've done. The If-Then Crapology diminishes the feelings of your Friend and almost says "I, and any normal person wouldn't have been hurt by my words/actions, but *you* are overly sensitive." It's like *you* telling someone to get over *them*selves! The exact opposite of a true apology.

By the way, we know we told you that our mantra is that YOU need to get over yourself. So what's wrong with passing on this wisdom to others when you're apologizing to them? This is different. Why? Because you bought this book, paying us to tell you to get over yourself. Nobody paid you to be rude!

Seriously, instead of telling your friend to get over it, let's go back to the Steps. Step Three asks you to imagine the impact of your actions on your friend. Step Four demands that you "Admit (let in) the Impact of Your Mistake On Them." Then, whether you think you know the effect of your actions or not, ask this question: "Is that how it was for *you*? If you'd like to tell me, I'd really like to know."

It might sound like this: "My friend, I imagine I hurt your feelings and made you angry when I (fill in the blank with what you did). Is that how it was for you? If you'd like to tell me, I'd really like to know."

This is our cure for the "If-Then Crapology." It acknowledges the validity of your Friend's feelings, rather than insinuating that they're a bozo for feeling that way.

A famous "if-then" apology is in Shakespeare's *A Midsummer Night's Dream*:

"If we shadows have offended/Think but this, and all is mended/That you have but slumber'd here . . . If you pardon, we will mend."

Essentially the character is saying, *If* we have upset you, just consider it a dream, and *if* you forgive us, we will make amends.

It's a beautiful and famous speech that comes at the end of a fantastical, almost psychedelic play, and, like all if-then apologies, it looks and sounds sincere, until you really think about what's being said!

Did Shakespeare know about this? Was he using the character as a kind of trickster? In the play, these words are spoken by Puck, a sprite. Is The Bard winking at us, more than 400 years later? We'll never know.

In any case, *your* life and the lives of others are not a psychedelic dream. Never resort to "If you are hurt, then I am sorry." That is, as perhaps the Bard would say, bullshit.

Kyte baby

A young American couple waiting on the birth of their adopted child was surprised by the baby's premature birth at twenty-two weeks. With their child in a neonatal unit hours away from their home, the young mother requested the chance to do her job remotely so she would be able to get to the hospital quickly.

The response the young couple received from CEO Ms. Ying Liu was a flat no.

The twist to the story? The company she works for, Kyte Baby, makes clothing for newborn kids. And guess what? The story went viral, with many people accusing the company of prejudice. Why? Because the child was adopted. People wondered if company policy favored birth parents over adoptive parents.

Like many crapologies, a second apology is necessary to clean up the mess of the first. The following is a great example of having to say sorry for an apology.

In her first apology, Kyte Baby CEO Ying Liu focused on the accusation of prejudice, which begs the question, 'where is the apology?'

"We treat biological and non-biological parents equally," Liu said. "Through my personal and professional experiences, I have the utmost respect for babies, families, and the adoption community."

This incredibly well-made non-sequitur drove the on-line community batty, inspiring them to make their feelings known with an avalanche of posts. And in the well-practiced tradition of having to apologize for one's apology, Ms. Liu's second message actually did a pretty good job of owning her mistake.

"Sincerely, what went wrong is how we treated Marissa and I'm the one who made the decision to veto her request to go remote as she stays in the NICU to take care of her adopted baby. When I think back, that was a terrible decision," Liu said. "I was insensitive, selfish and was only focused on the fact that her job had always been done on-site, and I didn't see the possibility of doing it remotely."

See what she did there? She said, *"I did X, I was being Y."* So great. Respect is due.

She expresses the way she was being (insensitive, selfish, etc.) and never blames those ways-of-being for her actions—denying a mother who is facing an emergency with some leeway in her work. There is a whole-ness to her ownership, she owns her actions and who she was being at the time. In other words, she has dominion over herself now.

Of course, more than this is necessary for freedom and happiness to show up for Ms. Liu, the parents and those concerned on the web. But she is on the right path, and we can expect the right things to follow. We almost don't want to criticize her at all, but the trick for you (and us) going forward is to pay attention to our apologies and to not have to apologize for them.

Don't Bother Apologizing If . . .

But are there times when you shouldn't apologize? You bet your ass!

Consider the following analogy: Zachary is in his late twenties and has just opened up a Roth retirement account, and after two years he has $14,000 in it. For Zack, that's a lot of money, but he will only realize the full value of the account if he keeps his grubby little fingers off it and follows the rules of the IRA. In his case, among other things, it means waiting until he is 59 and a half, when the investment has had a chance to mature before he benefits from it.

The same is true for the value of an apology, which carries the enormous promise of freedom and happiness. You don't have to wait until you are 67, but you still have to follow the rules of maturity that allow you to capture everything that an apology makes possible.

Simply said, our Six and a Half Steps ensure that you are as truthful as you can be, ensuring you have taken your broom to every corner and swept up every crumb that you can see. What follows are some of the times when you should absolutely not apologize. In each instance your apology will lack some critical piece. Your investment has yet to mature.

1. **Don't apologize if you aren't clear about your own mistakes.**

Sometimes we're blatantly aware that a relationship is in the toilet, broken, stuck, and we are convinced that if we made a good and honest apology, it would go some way toward getting things going again. The problem is, we honestly can't find anything to apologize for. This isn't us just trying to avoid the cringe factor, or the embarrassment of groveling; there are times when we just don't think we did anything wrong, or try as we might, we fail to see our mistakes.

Jason says:

I had a boss who was a high achiever and who had built a local radio station from scratch. My boss, let's call him Ted, gave me my first paid job in radio, after hearing me talk on a weekly show, which I did for fun, voluntarily. I was pretty good, if I say so myself, and I quickly became a kind of figurehead for the station. These were good times—my boss did an excellent job, I was having fun and felt like I was of service to the community.

For many reasons, my relationship with Ted began to strain. My boss and I began to avoid each other. I began to feel unappreciated and that everyone at the station was suffering under his leadership. My work was affected, and our relationship became untenable. In the end, I felt forced to quit my job.

I was sad to leave. I loved working at the station and I couldn't face Ted after that. I was angry with him.

Fortunately, my life moved on and other opportunities came my way, although deep down I missed being part of the little community radio station, which, shockingly, had been able to survive without me and my big microphone mouth.

I didn't like the way things had ended, and there was some resentment, but I moved on to other opportunities pretty quickly.

One of these opportunities came some years later, when Michael agreed to collaborate with me on this book. It was hard work at times but incredibly fulfilling.

A few months into the writing process, Michael asked me, "Did you ever talk to Ted?" "No," I replied, "I didn't. Why the hell should I? Ted is a dick." Michael was very quick to say that in that case I was a "fucking hypocrite. After all, you're writing a book about how to fix relationships through apology, for freedom and happiness!" I knew that the way I had responded to his initial question proved I was neither free nor happy.

"OK," I said, "but WTF am I apologizing for? I was a great DJ, a good interviewer, tremendous with the public . . . come on . . . what do I have to apologize for?" Michael thought for a while and finally said, "I don't know, but I think you should call him and ask him to meet—you'll figure it out."

I remember feeling sick. I remember cringing mightily. I certainly hadn't forgiven Ted for his transgressions as I saw them. The last thing I wanted to do was to call him for any reason, especially not to grovel to that bastard.

Even so, I knew that apologizing to Ted couldn't hurt either of us and that it just might help us to get unstuck in some way. I just truly didn't know what I had done.

I took the leap of faith. I called Ted and took our Second Step: I asked permission to meet and apologize. We agreed to meet in a week or so. I knew this would give me time to figure out how I was going to take the rest of The Six & A Half Steps.

Since Michael didn't know what I was to apologize for—thanks Mike, very helpful—I called my younger brother, Shel and asked him what he thought. Shel is a thoughtful and insightful guy, and, as my kid brother, nothing makes him happier than to make fun of me and to show me the error of my ways. I'm convinced it's his favorite thing to do in the world, apart from eating Chinese food on Christmas and going to Grateful Dead shows all year long. I told him my predicament and that I didn't know what I had done.

"Oh," said Shel. "I know what you did. You were an arrogant prick, and a lousy employee."

Lovely to hear. I hated that. Being accused of arrogance is an arrow in my Achilles Heel because I know it can be true, especially when I feel scared.

I'm sure I used some choice language to say he was wrong and that I'd been a great DJ and an asset to the station. Shel said, "I don't doubt it. I heard you, you were great, but look at your behavior from Ted's point of view. The more successful you got, the more self-important you became and the less likely you were to ask for advice. You were no longer a team player. You became a know-it-all and a bore. Any hope of humility and collaboration was lost in your stupid ego."

"Um, fabulous, Shel," I replied, dejected. My brother is good at this; I call it being "Shell-shocked." "How do you even know any of this is true? You weren't there!"
"Yes," said Shel. "I wasn't there, and I don't know Ted, but I do know *you.*"

I will tell you that the kind of trust I have in my brother and my love for him was hard won. It wasn't always so. We have both made many apologies to each other and many tears have been shed over the years. By the time of this conversation, I couldn't have found a Fairer Witness. He was right. I had been a really shitty employee. Arrogant and ungrateful. Snarky and belligerent. Now I knew what I was going to apologize for—in fact it seemed like a big nut to crack.

In the coming week, I talked again to Michael, and to Shel (who mostly called me a prick and laughed at me) and to a couple of other people I trust, including my wife, Ava, who actually was there while I was storming arrogantly, round the station.

Honestly, I still felt sick at the idea of the meeting. I really would rather have drunk my own vomit, but I knew I needed to do it, and I felt sufficiently disgusted at my own behavior to go through with it, even though I still thought Ted was a bastard who had ruined my radio career. I went nervously to meet Ted at a café in town and tearily told him what I realized I had done and how I imagined I had affected him. I asked the questions prescribed in this book and listened to his answers.

Dear reader: within five minutes I felt my body relax, a smile came to my face, and suddenly it was so great to see Ted. We'd shared so many really good times together. Very few people outside of Ted and I knew how it was in the early days of the radio station, overcoming technical, legal, and content crises. We were really sailing a weird little ship!

When I asked him if there was anything else I should take responsibility for, if I'd hurt him in ways I hadn't mentioned, you can bet he told me! Not my finest moment, and I cringed again to hear more of what I'd done and how I had made him and others feel. I took a breath, let what he had said sink in for a moment and apologized again.

Now, at this point in our conversation, a weight I didn't even know I was carrying was lifted from my life. Ted was visibly pleased, too; in fact, he took responsibility, in his own way, for the mistakes he made. It wasn't a Six and a Half Steps apology, but it was made in good faith and I loved him for it.

Looking back, I'm convinced that Ted felt able to forgive me and to make his own apology as the result of the freedom and happiness that was created by our meeting.

We had coffee. We laughed. He told me about his family. What a tremendous afternoon. Months later, Ted sold the station. When the new owner asked about me, Ted told him to call me. He said I was a big personality and could be a little bit of a loose cannon, but he could trust me to do the right things and to make things right when I fucked up.

I got my old job back and a bunch more responsibility to boot. I'm no longer working at the station, but that's another story for another time!

2. **Don't apologize without gaining your Friend's permission to do so.**

Why do we insist that to make an apology that really does its job of creating freedom and happiness, the apologizer should first make a call, (or contact their Friend in whatever way) and ask if they can apologize to them?

Because the apology isn't in what we say, *it's in what our Friend hears.*

This may seem like a no-brainer, but whenever we say anything to anyone, we are usually concerned with the words we're saying. We think that if we get the words right, they'll have the effect, great or small, that we intend. We tend to treat those words like we're posting something on social media. We say whatever's on our minds and hope that our intended impact will happen automatically.

Real conversation, a dialogue, is not like that at all. Especially the dialogue we call Apology. We are creating something valuable, and it takes two to tango.

We ought to be concerned, not so much with our words as we say them, but with how our apology will be received by our Friend. Even though we are the instigators, we want our Friend to be a part of the process from soup to nuts. By asking if they are interested in our apology, we immediately give our Friend agency. They get to decide whether they want to hang out with us at all. They can even ignore our call if they wish. There's no pressure on them.

If you are fortunate enough that they say yes, if they will listen to you, and if they'll even meet face to face with you, they are already a willing part of the process of healing the relationship, and both of you will get your chance to be a part of the creation of freedom and happiness.

But what happens if you ignore this advice? We like the metaphor of a full teacup. What happens if you try to pour more tea into it? It spills over, it's wasted, it's all over the table, and some of it is in your lap. If your Friend is too "full" to hear your apology, like the tea, it's wasted and it's likely to be messy. *Remember our Golden Rule of not making things worse.*

3. **Don't apologize if you can't clearly say "I did X, and I was being Y."**

Here's a bold statement: the human brain is designed to exaggerate its owner's goodness and minimize any badness.

Again, what do we know? We're not neuroscientists, and honestly, we're arrogant enough to have not bothered to interview one for this book. So, why are we so cocky?

We've lived many decades in self-examination and we know what it is to be backed into a corner by our own mistakes. Many times we have had to face our personal failings and the ways we defend ourselves in the face of criticism.

This instinct, this reflex, is the reason why Jason was unable to see what he had done to Ted in the story above. He was protecting himself by exaggerating his own goodness (he was a great DJ) while shrinking his mistakes to the point of making them invisible (to himself).

So, don't bother to apologize . . .

- if you're not ready to be brutally honest with yourself, or, like Jason, ask someone to do it for you.
- if, when you discover the Uninvited Guest of how you were being at the time of your mistake, you're not ready to share it with your Friend.

- if you're still desperate to say WHY you did what you did, or to blame your behavior on someone or something, including your Uninvited Guest.

4. **Don't apologize until you're in the other person's shoes.**

OK, so you're sorry. Good. We know how you feel. You did or said something shitty and you feel remorse. And, you don't want to feel that way anymore. You wish you could turn back the clock and not have said or done the shitty thing. This is great. You have human feelings and are probably not a sociopath. The thing is, you know by now that your sorrow is just that, *yours*. The same applies to your remorse, your guilt, your shame, or whatever uncomfortable feelings you're trying to escape.

The problem is, in an apology, the more we focus on our own feelings, the less likely we are to have any effect on them. It's well known (and has been said by many great thinkers) that the one sure way to make yourself miserable is to chase happiness. Ask any alcoholic!

If your focus is for the most part on resolving your remorse, you are still in your own shoes, when, as you know, you should be considering the effects your behavior has had on your Friend. You can't be in two places at once.

Step Four demands that you admit (let in) the impact of *your* mistakes on *them*. Your feelings are in response to the impact of your mistakes on *you*, not them.

Our goal here is to place ourselves in the shoes of our Friend and truly admit how our behavior made *them* feel. Strangely, when we really express to our Friends the impact we made on them with our mistakes, we start to feel better with no focus on our own feelings.

Bottom line, wait to apologize until you are fully in their world and it's not all about you. You do this by applying our Steps, doing the appropriate soul searching, talking with your Fair Witness and making the call.

5. **Don't apologize if you cannot be trusted to keep your promises.**

Why is making a promise an important step? Relationships break down when people's behavior begins to form cracks in the fabric of what is possible going forward. Whether at work with a manager, or with family, or close friends, we pull away from each other when we are unhappy with the future we envision with those people. Why would we bother hanging out somewhere or with someone if we think it's never going to get better?

We went to our friend the Internet and typed in the phrase "I don't see a future with . . ." leaving it open-ended. Dozens of pages full of instances appeared with headlines like . . .

- I can't see a future with you
- I love you so much, but I don't see a future
- Here's how to tell someone you don't see a future with them
- He said he doesn't see a future with you
- 13 Concrete signs that he doesn't see a future with you
- What to do when you love them but don't see a future

And on and on . . .

It's really amazing to see how much the future we envision determines how we feel about today and how we behave. The workweek is such a great example. Why do we have the Monday morning blues? Why is Wednesday hump day, and why does the eagle fly on Friday?

It's very common to spend a great deal of time discussing our distant past. Our childhoods clearly are of interest to us and the possibility that they are having profound effects on our current lives. Less often do we focus on how we feel about the future. What are you doing next Wednesday? Are you hopeful?

Just as important to us than our past or even the present we find ourselves in are our beliefs, hopes, and fears about what the future holds. We walk toward the future we believe in and are committed to, more than the hardships we stand in today. If we promise ourselves and our communities that the future is one of freedom and happiness, our lives become hopeful. Our Steps follow the hope we hold, more than the struggle we carry.

Hang on a minute. Aren't we here to mend what was broken in the *past*? Yes, absolutely! But that's only the first step in creating a new path forward. A new future at work that can bring out the best the team can do. A new future in your family that can inspire compassion and affection. A new future with your Friends built on trust.

The promises we make in Step Five actually create a new future with our Friends. And when those promises are kept, that future just gets more and more amazing.

A friend of ours used to say, "A little hope goes a long way." When we make a promise, we create hope.

How nice. Sadly, that lovely warm feeling of hope is very fragile. When a promise is broken, hope can be dashed so very brutally against the rocks. In *that* future, you are not to be trusted. People are anxious and unhappy around you, and you are defensive and glum.

So what new path, what new relationship do you want to create?

A kept promise creates the possibility that things are indeed going to get better. It manifests as freedom and happiness and it's incredibly powerful.

When Elton John sings "Sorry Seems To Be The Hardest Word," we all know exactly what he means. Saying sorry sucks. We all hate admitting our mistakes, especially with the people who are the most important to us. We hate making mistakes and we hate being wrong. Even the most experienced apologizer can expect to feel uncomfortable when taking the Six and a Half Steps, and sometimes our instinct is to get out of there as quickly as possible. This is another example of our brains being in protection mode. Don't make rash promises just to escape a feeling.

Ask what your Friend needs going forward, for things to be right between you. Make a promise based on their response, but don't fall down the common rabbit hole of making a promise you can't keep.

If you owe someone $100, don't promise to pay them $10 a month if you know it's likely you won't always be able to. What about December? You'll have the kids' presents to buy. Be honest. Better to promise $1 and to make the payments. Promise and plan to be trustworthy.

This is exactly how to build this new future with your Friend.

6. **Don't apologize if you're not ready to grow.**

> Michael says: When I was sixty I weighed 160 lbs.; at seventy I weighed 180 lbs. This is not the personal growth we are talking about.

In fact, earlier we promised you'd *lose* 50 lbs. of psychic weight by apologizing.

First off, let's talk a little about our perfect imperfections. We have been told all our lives that we need to get at least just a little better. A little smarter, a little stronger, a little more compassionate, a little more wealthy, a little more good-looking. And some of us have been told we need to get a *lot* better, not just a little.

In fact, you could say our consumer culture begins with the premise that you and I are not OK as is. If we had a better job, car, toothpaste, education, friends etc., *then* we'd be alright. If you go to the bookstore and peruse the self-help aisle, you'll notice that tons of the books refer to personal growth. So many of these books imply and reinforce the sense that there's something wrong with us. If only we could self-help ourselves, we'd be OK.

But none of that is what we mean by growth, and in fact we think that everyone, including you and I, is *perfectly imperfect*.

So then, what can growth really be about if there's nothing wrong with you? In fact, if there's nothing wrong with you, why would you want to take on personal growth? What does it even mean to change something about yourself if you are exactly the way you're supposed to be anyway? And if growth *is* desirable, how does one attain it?

> The problem with self-help and personal growth is that they are usually attempted in the context of something being wrong with us. The more we fix ourselves, the more we reinforce the concept that we need to be fixed.

Just consider weight loss or being loved. If we think we are too heavy, can we ever lose enough weight? If we think we are unlovable, can we ever see the love around us? This is the proverbial vicious circle of personal growth.

What we're getting at is something we think is important for us to acknowledge; there is nothing wrong with you. You make mistakes. That's all. And, in this way, you are not at all exceptional—*human beings are mistake-making machines.*

What is the concept of personal growth about when it's not about fixing ourselves? Perhaps growth can be a way to express what inspires us about life. Are you energized by having a dumb, hot-headed argument and then storming off, or does open and honest communication inspire you? Then take it on. Are you content to be mediocre with a dash of fear-driven laziness, or does excellence inspire you? Then take it on.

Of course, our silly descriptions of being dumb, lazy, and mediocre mentioned above, are just our way of getting your attention. These types of words are from the world of self-improvement. We consider every human being to be perfectly imperfect as they are.

Get involved in whatever breathes life into you. That's what we mean by taking on what inspires you.

What gets you going? What in the world fascinates you? What moves you? This Easter egg hunt for inspiration can be inspiring in and of itself!

But avoid taking on ANYTHING that reinforces that you just aren't enough as you are. Rather than wasting time and energy focusing on what you think is wrong with you, embark on a journey to discover what in life inspires you. In this way personal growth becomes the pathway to a life that fills you with joy, instead of a pathway to a life that proves you aren't enough.

And this goes double for the desire we all have to change other people: our husband, our wife, our boss, our employees, our children and the whole damn world. See what happens when you put that to the side and find out what inspires you about them.

Before we get off this crazy world of inspiration, get this: when we fix a broken relationship with an apology and become free and happy as the result, we begin to see people differently. In our experience, we judge our fellows less and begin to find them fascinating. They begin, in fact, to inspire us. Even people we've known for years.

We spend a lot less time worrying about how things, other people and ourselves could and should be different and we enjoy the world as it is: perfectly imperfect.

This is the type of growth we are inviting you to take on.

Practically speaking, how the hell does someone grow? By Practice.

Jason has been a professional musician for forty years, and his performance today is light years away from the first time he picked up his guitar. What does a professional pilot do before every take off? She goes through the same take-off procedure she has done hundreds of times before. Why do doctors have rigorous years-long internship and residency in their field before they are legally certified? Why do musicians also quip, "how do you get to Carnegie Hall? Practice!"

The point we are making here is that taking action in real life over and over again is the way we attain the experience, the wisdom, and the skills necessary to make a difference.

The same is true for an apology. Training yourself to make an effective apology and then being committed to its practice, day in and day out, is what gives you the freedom and happiness we promise.

This is especially true, when in Step Six we have asked our Friend if there's anything more we can do to make things right for them and made promises about our actions in the future. As time goes by, and as our promises remain unbroken, we have, by definition, grown.

Successful apologies set everyone involved free, but what does that freedom look like? There are as many answers to this question as there are people who apologize, but even while we're still applying the Six and a Half Steps to an apology to a Friend, a clear example of growth presents itself.

And it's entirely possible that you are completely unaware of the growth that's occurred for you so far. This is our favorite kind of growth, the kind we're not aware of, the kind we can't be smug about.

In Step Six we ask our Friend, after making a promise for the future, what more we can do to make things right *for them*. Their answer, whatever it is, will provide a fantastic opportunity to express the growth we've had during the process of apologizing.

If they say, "No—we're good, there's nothing more to do," we just leave the door open to them to change their mind down the road. If they make a request, we get to make a decision, based on our newfound freedom and happiness. Without fear, or greed, or any bad feeling at all, we now have the kind of authorship of our lives some people only dream of. We get to say yes, or no, or maybe, or I'll get back to you, or let me talk to my wife/kids/boss/dad/mechanic/butcher/yoga instructor . . .

And again, this is not a one-shot deal. Like anything worthwhile, from buying flowers for your mother, to playing in an orchestra, to running the marathon, a lifetime of practice is required. And, as any ninety-year-old son, pianist, or runner will tell you, you never quite get "perfect."

Carnegie Hall is still a ways away, but we're closer and we're enjoying the journey.

Practice makes imperfect—perfectly.

Step Six and a Half: Don't apologize if you are expecting to be forgiven right away.

In fact, in life, the discomfort we feel in the gap between what happens and what we thought would happen can be measured by our expectations.

Making an apology is time consuming and it can be an emotional process. It requires courage to really look at ourselves and to honestly confess our shortcomings to our Friends, our loved ones and our acquaintances. To make and keep promises requires elbow grease and stamina.

Perhaps because of the effort it takes, it is understandable if we have expectations of the outcome. It would be natural to expect or really want our Friend to forgive us, to say they understand, to offer to buy lunch, or do anything else to make us feel better.

This is a wild goose chase if ever there was one.

When we have made our apology, after the first six steps are complete, there's our beautiful little half step. This may seem flippant, or something just attached to the end to catch the reader's eye, or an attempt to stand out from the apology crowd. Well, we're not that smart.

Our Step Six and a Half is much bigger than it looks. It says "don't push it" because we know how incredibly tempting it can be to call our Friends and try to elicit a follow-up conversation. To see how we did. To feel better. To look good. We're growing, but we're still perfectly imperfect.

Like us, once in a while you might feel a very strong urge to ignore this step. Maybe it's calling out to you. You can't sleep, or you're calling your Fair Witness every hour . . . notice how addicted you are, like us, to looking good and feeling better.

So what to do? This is your chance to be a Zen master! The time after an apology is intense. These expectations and thoughts of all kinds are bound to spin around your head. Notice them. Find a practice that works for you. Write them down, even *before* you make your apology. Have a conversation with a Fair Witness about them. Meditate. Laugh at yourself. Eat a donut. The important thing is that you don't act out on your expectations, and never, never put them in between you and your friend.

Part Three: Beyond the Steps

FORGIVENESS

"If we can forgive what's been done to us . . . If we can forgive what we've done to others . . . If we can leave our stories behind, our being victims and villains, only then can we maybe rescue the world."

—Chuck Palahniuk

"Whatever you're pissed off at me about, just forgive me already so we can move on."

—Quote from a mom to her daughter

In the process of writing this book, we've shared our thoughts and notes with the people close to us, people we love and respect, to get their feedback. Almost every person asks us what we have to say about forgiveness.

This is completely understandable, as apology and forgiveness seem like two sides of a coin.

So first off, what is this thing we call forgiveness?

One of the most common definitions of forgiveness can be found in the American Psychological Association's dictionary: (Forgiveness is) "willfully putting aside feelings of resentment toward an individual who has committed a wrong, been unfair or hurtful, or otherwise harmed one in some way. Forgiveness is not equated with reconciliation or excusing another, and it is not merely accepting what happened or ceasing to be angry."

This is really a great definition, and it underlines the fact that you don't have to forget to forgive. You don't have to excuse or even accept someone's words or actions in order to forgive them. But, knowing what something is and doing it are two very different things. You can know about pole vaulting and have a step-by-step manual for it—you can even own your own pole, but pole vaulting itself is (presumably) a very different thing altogether.

Here is a less technical definition of forgiveness:

"Forgiveness is giving up all hope for a better past."
—Actress Lily Tomlin

We love this metaphor very much. It may or may not resonate with you, perhaps because it is not the "how" of forgiveness. It describes the nature of forgiveness without giving a hint of methodology. We'd all be delighted if whatever hurt us hadn't happened at all, and we certainly wish we could be big enough to let go of the pain—but exactly how does one do that?

Throughout this book, we've been careful to give only two desired outcomes from an effective apology: Freedom and Happiness. We never promised anything more or less than those two things. Not wishing to sound like a broken record, let's say it again. We're learning this incredible practice in order *to create Freedom and Happiness for ourselves and others*. We're not doing it for any other purpose—not even forgiveness. That's not to say that we definitely won't get some; we may also get a piece of cheesecake, but we're not doing it for that, either.

Even so, the question of forgiveness is important, and we are going to say a few words about it here, from the perspective of what it takes for *you* to forgive someone, whether they apologize to you or not. And we'll address what to do if they apologize, whether they do it perfectly or even if they make a terrible, crappy apology, in other words, a Crapology.

Crapology. Earlier, we quipped that we're sorry that we're not sorry for coining this word. We do, however, realize that it may be annoying to some folks. Knowing ourselves and our juvenile sense of humor, we acknowledge that this may be at least some of the point. Aside from being childish, it also has another possibly troubling effect. If, as an educated apologizer, you are fortunate enough to have someone apologize to you, it may be tempting to judge that apology in light of the information contained in this book. You may think something like, "wow, that was a terrible apology. It misses the mark by miles. It's definitely what Michael and Jason would call a 'Crapology.'"

Here's our suggestion. Look for signs the person means well and accept all apologies with grace and gratitude. You know as well as anyone that they're not easy to make, so be willing to forgive. A good way to achieve this, to negate any judgment you may have arrived at, is to say to yourself, "that may be as good as I'm going to get here. This person is doing their best. I'm grateful."

So, whatever we tell ourselves about a person, their actions or motivations, we suggest that there is a path to forgiving them. Being completely Zen about it isn't your only option. It can work; however, there is another practical way to help your Friend get the Crapology off his shoes.

When someone attempts an apology that falls short of our Six and a Half Steps, we try to respond graciously and understand that whatever they say may be the best we can expect.

After all, our apologizer is, like us, perfectly imperfect. We strongly encourage you to practice courteous goodwill in the face of a Crapology, but we also know that people's best efforts are often less than satisfying.

"I'm sorry if I upset you" may be the best someone can do at that moment, but it hardly creates much in the way of freedom or happiness. There's so much that is unsaid in some apologies that can leave people walking away grumbling or wondering whether they ever want to speak to each other again. A poor apology adds to the confusion. It makes things worse.

On the other hand, when an apology is fully expressed and well made, everyone feels more satisfied.

We say it's possible to help your Friend apologize more fully, leaving you both in better shape, without being patronizing or cruel.

Our experience tells us that you can apply our Steps in a creative way to have a satisfying conversation that benefits everyone. We've done some of this work for you by coming up with a set of possible questions you can ask your Friend, based on elements from the Six and a Half Steps.

So, when someone makes a less-than-satisfying apology to you, take a breath and consider the following questions. If you don't like any of them, feel free to make up your own. At the very least, they are food for thought.

From Step One: Know and Own Your Mistakes

If the person is not really telling you what they did, or if they are burying what they did in a ton of reasons, you can ask:

- I'm not sure what you're apologizing for. Could you be clearer?
- I understand and appreciate your rationale, but can we focus on what you did?

From Step Two: Ask Permission to Apologize

If the person didn't ask your permission to apologize, or if you weren't expecting them to apologize in the moment (if they accost you in the supermarket or show up at your door), you could ask:

- Would you mind if we talked about this at a later time? Can we schedule it? I want to take this seriously, and I'm not really ready at the moment to fully listen.

If your Friend seems annoyed while making the apology, you could ask:

- Are you upset with me? Do you think I played a part in this? Is there something I need to take responsibility for? It may be we both have something to apologize for. Let's discuss it.

From Step Three: Say "I Am Really Sorry"

If your friend apologizes for what they did and you want to deepen the conversation, you could give them a chance to say how they were being at the time of the incident.

You could say:

- Thank you, I appreciate you saying sorry. It's good to hear you take responsibility for what you did. How were you feeling at the time?

Without getting into the weeds of "I did X, I was being Y" with your Friend, this simple question can open up a conversation that gets to the measure of it.

From Step Four: Admit the Impact of Your Mistake on Them

If you don't feel that your Friend has truly considered the effect of their behavior on you, you could ask:

- How do you think that made me feel?
- Do you think there might be other repercussions? Could anyone else have been affected?

From Step Five: Promise You Can Be Trusted in the Future

If your Friend doesn't make clear to you how they are going to clean up the mess made by their mistake, you could ask:

- Well, what are you going to do about this? What could you do to make this right?

If you don't get the sense that your Friend can be trusted in the future, you can ask:

- How are you not going to make this mistake again? What are you going to put into place to make sure?

From Step Six: Ask If You Can Do Anything More

- Would you be open to doing this . . . (say what you need in order to be fully satisfied)? This would really put the issue to bed for me.

From Step Six and a Half Don't Push It

If, after your friend has made their apology, they keep asking if you forgive them, you could say:

- I am grateful for everything you said and I appreciate everything you had to go through to have this great conversation with me. Thank you for listening to me. Now I have a request: would you give me some time to consider if there's anything more about this we should discuss? I'll get back to you when I'm ready.

As an end to this section, we have an important caveat: you know your people and we don't. These suggested questions and the ideas behind them are by no means obligatory—in fact, they could backfire spectacularly, especially if your Friend is not ready to hear them. Folks often come to make an apology expecting to make their speech and walk away. In fact, it's not uncommon for someone to make an apology with the attitude that *you* should be grateful that they're even talking to you, let alone groveling! It may be a shock to them that an apology is a conversation—a two-way street. We suggest testing the water with just one of the questions first and seeing how it's received. Your tone will make an enormous difference. So, if it seems to make things worse, back off. Again: your Friend's attempt at apology may be the best you can expect, and we suggest you accept it with grace.

NOW, we are ready to talk about forgiveness, regardless of the situation, Apology, Crapology, or no apology at all.

We say how-to-forgive comes down to two actions: Getting and Giving.

1. Getting (fully understanding, admitting) that given the right circumstances, you could behave as badly as the person who hurt you.
2. Giving up the *advantage* of being resentful.

Let's begin with #1: Getting.

Here's a trick question: If you were the person who hurt you, in the same set of circumstances, with their education, experience, economics etc., could you have done what they did?

Some folks might immediately answer, "No! What they did was unconscionable! How dare you even suggest that I'm capable of such behavior!"

Slow down, Pardner. Clearly, if you *were* them (with their set of circumstances, etc.) you *could* do what they did. It's a trick question. It's like asking if you were a chicken, could you cluck and lay an egg?

Now here's a follow-up, non-trick question: have you ever done something really shitty to someone? Something you weren't proud of? Something that makes you cringe to remember even to this day? Of course you have! We all have. It's part of being human. And none of us is the personification of evil: one who will never deserve to be forgiven.

This first step of Getting, or internalizing that given the right circumstances, you could behave as badly as the person who hurt you, is recognizing our shared humanity, both in the dark corners of our soul and where the light does shine through. While people talk about compassion, this is actually where the rubber meets the road. Recognizing our shared humanity is the root of all effective forgiveness.

If we're correct, and behaving from time to time in ways that hurt others is part of being human, and if we hope that folks will forgive us for *our* humanity, then we suggest that it follows that we have an obligation to find ways to do the same for others.

The word "resentment" literally means "to feel again." Long after someone has wronged us, we recall the act and feel the pain of it, often in ways that have little to do with what *actually* happened. Our part of it shrinks—we become more angelic and faultless and What-They-Did becomes more heinous and hurtful. We play the role of the innocent lamb and the other guy becomes a pantomime villain.

Why do we do this? It's clearly not a successful strategy, if it's a strategy at all. We can go on reliving and expanding the pain of something (that may or may not have happened in the way we recall it) for our entire lives. And this pain can represent numerous obstacles to our own freedom and happiness. What's it all about?

Somewhere along the road, there are other consequences of resentment. Not only pain. And these consequences can be felt in some bizarre way as positive for a long, long time. Even though inevitably, these positive consequences eventually turn sour. It's The Law of Diminishing Returns.

The Story of Michael's Mom, Freida.

My mom was one of four sisters, Mabel, Sadie, Freida, and Grace. Mabel and Sadie lived next door to us with their mom, Dora, and Grace moved to Washington, DC, where she married and had a family. Until I was ten years old, Grace's family was very much a part of ours—we visited them, they visited us, and I got to know and love my DC cousins. Then something happened.

Mabel, Sadie, and my mom, Freida, stopped talking to Grace and suddenly that part of our family just disappeared. No more visits to DC where my older girl cousins would take me for rides in their convertible, while blasting The Beatles on the radio. I loved them and I was crushed. As a ten-year-old I had no understanding of what had happened, nor was I offered any explanation.

As the years passed, I began to hear dribs and drabs of conversations between my mom and Aunts Mabel and Sadie. I would hear the complaints they had about Grace. As far as I could tell, they felt Grace wasn't holding up her side of taking care of my Grandma, who lived with Sadie and Mabel. To me, as a ten-year-old, this seemed to be the reason for the loss of my DC family. Rightly or wrongly, my mom and aunts' story about Grace justified cutting them off.

Freida was angry with Grace, but she also felt acute sadness over the loss of her relationship with her sister. But for Freida, it was Grace who was responsible for the whole thing.

Freida had a "dead-to-me" sister, not to mention a brother-in-law and two nieces in DC. And this went on for fifteen long, angry, and painful years.

So, Mom had lost a lot, and she had the pain, anger, and sadness that came with that loss. But there were some other things that came along with that loss. She had a really good reason and a lot of righteous indignation. And here's the kicker: all that drama made a secret of the fact that it was *her* decision to kill the relationship, not Grace's. The benefit of Freida's resentment was she didn't have to be responsible for not speaking to Grace. And, this gave her an advantage in the relationship. She could "enjoy" feeling superior at a distance from her sister without having to rationalize it to anyone but herself and her co-conspirators, Mabel and Sadie. She didn't have to own her part in the drama.

Fifteen years into this, when I was twenty-five years old, Mom came to me and said, "I've just invited Grace to dinner. What do you think I ought to say?"

I was dumbfounded. This was miraculous. It was as if Moses had just parted the Red Sea in front of me. I could not imagine what had inspired such a reunion and when asked, here's what Mom said: "It's not worth losing a sister over."

In other words, Freida saw how she was benefiting from her resentment and decided the price was too much. She gave up that benefit for the chance that all of us could be a loving family again. Mom gave up her feelings about Grace's selfishness and got back her sister. She had killed the relationship all those years ago and now she was breathing life back into it. The fact is: she just couldn't stand it anymore. This is a gift. It's what some people in 12-Step programs call "The gift of desperation."

This story is meant to shed light on our second action of forgiveness: Giving. Consider that not forgiving becomes addictive as we bask in our self-righteousness. Like most addictions, of course, it eventually stops getting us high and starts kicking our ass. And, as Freida said, "it's just not worth it anymore." Being willing to give up the advantage of resentment is the second necessary step in forgiveness. And you don't have to wait fifteen years to become willing. You can become willing now.

Here's the rub: how do you know with certainty that you are willing, Grasshopper? You know you are willing when you have picked up the phone and are dialing the number.

> "Three frogs on a log.
> One decides to jump off.
> How many frogs on the log?
> Three frogs on a log."
> (ancient parable)

Again, forgiveness is composed of two steps. First, we *get* that all of us are human, and we all do stupid shit, you included. Next, we *give* up the diminishing returns of holding on to the self-righteous anger and blame that are holding us back from the freedom and happiness of good relationships.

And so, just as we had to get over our discomfort in order to make that first call in our apology, we may have to wade through some of our own tightly held beliefs, feelings and opinions to be willing to forgive. Again, expect to cringe in the service of freedom and happiness. In this way, the process of forgiving can be much like the process of apologizing.

Forgiveness and apology are both about personal responsibility.

When we apologize, we never mention the actions of our Friend, only our own actions. We neither blame circumstances nor our Friend, nor any*one* or any*thing* for what-we-did. This is what we mean by personal responsibility. In an apology, we own our actions and the impact of those actions. Even more importantly, we own our own *lives* in this manner.

Similarly, when we forgive, however we achieve it, no one other than ourselves is accountable for that forgiveness. There have been times when someone has "apologized" to us in the most horrible manner and we forgave. There have been times when someone apologized to us in a textbook perfect way and we forgave. There have also been times when someone *never* apologized to us at all and we forgave. To be honest, we aren't saints, and there have been times in our lives when we have been unforgiving in the face of any type of apology. You, too, may have found yourself in similar situations.

In each case, it was up to us to forgive or not. An apology doesn't cause forgiveness. We forgive or not, and never is it dependent on the apology. That is personal responsibility in the Land of Forgiveness.

Of course, we are convinced that a well-made apology creates Freedom and Happiness for all parties involved. Even more, the ripple effect can be positive for their entire community. When someone apologizes well, it creates the opportunity for the recipient to be more free and happy, and that can leave them with an increased desire and ability to forgive.

The trick here is to forgive others regardless of the quality, as we judge it, of *their* contrition or their apology, if any. So, it doesn't matter if or how someone apologizes to us. If we are interested in Freedom and Happiness, we find a way to forgive them.

This doesn't mean they are free to do us harm in the future, or that we shouldn't be cautious, for example, to lend money to a drug addict! Forgiveness doesn't mean we approve of their actions or could accept the same behavior in the future.

By the way: feel free not to forgive. Do what you want. If you disagree, fine. But how do you feel? Nothing changes unless something changes.

> *"Not forgiving is like drinking rat poison and waiting for the rat to die."*
>
> —Anne Lamott

> *"The weak do not forgive. Forgiveness is an attribute of the strong."*
>
> —Mahatma Gandhi

> *"As I walked out the door toward the gate that would lead to my freedom, I knew if I didn't leave my bitterness and hatred behind, I'd still be in prison."*
>
> —Nelson Mandela

SINCERITY IS WEAK TEA

"When deeds speak, feelings are silent."

—African proverb

"My feelings are very ambitious; my actions less so."

—Anonymous

Another topic that regularly raises its head when we talk to our friends about apology, is sincerity. Sometimes folks ask us how we know that the apologizer is sincere; that is to say, how we can believe that they mean what they say. Sometimes people even ask how *they* could know that *they themselves* are sincere in their desire to apologize.

We totally understand the concern about sincerity. After all, we're taught as kids that when we "apologize" to someone we should "mean it," and "feel" sorry. On top of this, we are often told by our parents or teachers to go and apologize to someone. They are often correct! Perhaps we should say we are sorry, but how can we mean it when we are being told to?

So much of our strategies, attitudes, and beliefs about how to correct our mistakes came to us as children from our parents and teachers. Because they cared deeply about us, they were hoping to shape us into decent human beings with great relationships and to help us avoid the mistakes they themselves had made. All of this advice and instruction was, of course, understood and processed through the mind of a child and brought with us into adult situations, years later. For an adult, some of this stuff is just not useful anymore.

Of course, when we're being told by someone to apologize, we seldom *do* mean it! The idea of apologizing didn't come from us. We are, to some degree, being forced to say sorry, so how could we really mean it? At that point we probably aren't even close to being ready to apologize. Not in the way we describe in this book. We certainly would not yet have seen whatever is upsetting our Friend from *their* point of view, including and especially how what we might have done had caused that upset. No one likes to be forced to do anything. How would *you* feel? Would you make a good job of it?

While it's not one of the Six and a Half Steps, if there was a step-zero, or a fundamental truth underlying the Steps, it would be that you don't HAVE TO apologize to anyone for anything if you don't want to. If you do, you may break Jason and Michael's Golden Rule: Don't Make Things Worse.

This is the freedom of choice that allows your apology to have real power, when you put it to use. It's also the opening we create that allows something other than sincerity to sneak in the back door. Read on.

You don't have to feel anything in particular, other than a desire to create more freedom and more happiness for yourself and your Friends!

Jason says:

"The City of Laguna Beach, California, is a popular tourist destination, especially in the summertime. Frankly, the place gets packed—hordes of visitors and locals, masses of cars, and parking becomes impossible. One of the main streets downtown, Forest Avenue, once a traffic thoroughfare, was closed off to cars some years ago and is now a lovely pedestrian walkway, lined with trees, stores, and restaurants, ending at the beach. At one end of the no-car-zone is a small stage, used by musicians, curated by The City. I've been booked there many times, to sit in the sunshine and sing and play guitar to people on a patio of tables and chairs opposite. In the cooler months, loading my equipment is easy. I just pull up at the end of the street, take the speakers, amp, stands, guitar, and cables to the stage. I have a friend watch it all while I park the car nearby. The summer is a different story . . .

One time, in July, I arrived for work to find Laguna particularly insane. People everywhere, cars bumper to bumper. At the end of Forest Ave. there stood a group of volunteer traffic cops, attempting to keep the flow, well . . . flowing. My long-suffering wife, Ava, was driving. She pulled up to park the car to let me unload and one of the cops motioned for us to keep moving. I wound the window down and asked him where he'd like me to unload for my gig. "Not here," he said. "Where then?" said I—feeling my blood beginning to boil. "I don't care. But you can't stay here—there's a line of cars behind you!" At this point I lost my mind. I called the guy a dick and dropped a few F-bombs to boot. Ava pulled away as I yelled hysterically out the window from an increasing distance.

She found a safe place to stop the car, if not park, close by, pulled over, and looked me in the eye. "Jason Feddy," she said, eyes wide open, "that was NOT COOL! I hate it when you behave like that. Go and apologize to that guy. You're being an asshole." I knew she was right, but I was embarrassed. I know how I can be when I'm angry (and scared—I didn't want to be late for my gig or have to carry my gear a long way). I get arrogant and self-righteous and loud. I stop listening. Shit. I hate it when I behave like that too. "OK, OK, I'm sorry, sheesh," I mumbled and got out of the car with my stuff. If Ava, the cop, and I were to have a chance at happiness and freedom from this ridiculous display of mine, I knew what I had to do.

Still fuming with self-righteous indignation and now embarrassment, I put my equipment on the stage and went over to where the volunteer cop was standing. During a slight break in the traffic I said, "Sir . . ." He turned to face me, "I want to apologize to you for raising my voice and using horrible language. You have a tough and important job here and I was disruptive and rude. I'm sorry." "Yes," he said, and before I had a chance to ask if there was anything else, he said, "I'm a volunteer here, just trying to keep the traffic flowing. You can see how difficult it can be. Please follow our instructions."

Still seething and full of the kind of adrenaline only embarrassment can generate, I wanted to deck the guy. It took all my strength to keep my mouth shut, but I did. I said, "You got it, sir, once again, I'm really sorry." He said thanks, and he was grateful for my apology. He smiled and I (kinda) did too.

I set up for the gig and my adrenaline subsided. I relaxed. A few minutes later, Ava appeared with Barklee, our dog. She'd found parking a little ways away. "Did you apologize to that bloke?" "Yes," I said, "And Ave, I'm really sorry to have put you through that madness. I wasn't sorry when I said it in the car, but I am now." Ever the philosopher, Ava said, "Just don't fucking do it again!"

Here's the thing, and it's not conventional wisdom: while I wasn't being sincere in the old sense of the word, acting true to one's feelings (I apologized even though I was still fuming), my apology was entirely honest. How do we explain that?

As Jason points out, the common everyday understanding of sincerity is the act of behaving consistently with how we feel.

Over the years we have found that how we feel isn't really all that important, and in fact, we may not have much say in how we actually feel. Our feelings may be like the English weather—one minute it's hot, then cold, then rain, then sleet and fog. In the end we stand there wishing we had an umbrella. In other words, our feelings may be something that happens to us.

In this world, Jason would be sincere only if he felt sorry at the moment of the apology. Fortunately, we are not really interested in sincerity.

What matters, and what works here, is being true.

Sincerity and truthfulness are not the same thing. If being sincere is acting consistent with our feelings, then what is being true?

> Truthful behavior is acting consistently with our commitments. By that we mean, if we represent ourselves to the world as a caring person, then being true is being caring, even if we don't feel like it at the moment.

Are you committed to being a jerk? If so, then strange as it seems, truthfulness would be acting like a jerk!

Why the distinction between sincerity and truthfulness? Because as we said earlier, we may not have much say in the matter of our feelings. However, we *always* have a say in the matter of who we are committed to being in life. In Jason's example, he was sincere when he was yelling at the cop! He really, really, really *felt* angry and justified in expressing it all.

On the other hand, Jason had already promised his friends and his family that he was committed to the freedom and happiness of himself and others. He now had a choice that he didn't have before he declared who he was.

Now, he could choose to act based on his sincere feelings or he could choose to act true to his promise.

When Jason first told Ava he would apologize, he definitely didn't *fee*l like it. When he walked over to the officer, he felt like it a little more but not all the way. By his own admission, he still "wanted to deck the guy." After the officer had a chance to express himself and forgive Jason, it really didn't matter that Jason didn't feel like it when he approached the copper. The result was freedom and happiness for both of them. Ava saw Jason hear her and take responsibility for his actions. Finally, Jason was able to perform for his audience well, without the lingering stress and embarrassment of the interaction. The ripple effects from this tiny, truthful apology went on and on. For one thing, Jason is still being booked to play on Forest Avenue. If that isn't a trimtab, what is?

We must, however, acknowledge that there are times when our feelings are overwhelming—when they completely take us over. Neuroscientists call this the "Amygdala Hijack," and it happens when something occurs as a threat to our survival. In these "fight or flight" moments, we are *reacting*, and we'll often do something we may later regret. In those moments we really don't have much of a choice in the matter.

We all have had a lifetime of reacting, but how much time have we actually spent letting our friends, family and colleagues know who we are committed to being? We have seen in our experience of working with individuals and groups that practicing having that kind of conversation with our friends begins to balance our reactions with our intentions, giving us more choice when our feelings become overwhelming.

We're not neurologists or psychologists, and we're not psychics. We're not mind readers, so we have no way of telling a person's level of sincerity, reliability, honesty, or integrity. The good news is, if you have found yourself in a broken or stuck relationship, and you want to fix it, sincerity is irrelevant.

Our experience shows that if you have done the necessary soul searching, if you are prepared in the ways that we have laid out here, and are sitting nervously in a café, waiting for your friend to meet you, or standing at the side of the road hoping to catch the attention of a traffic cop, your feelings will be whatever they are. It's the process that matters, *not how you feel.*

That's the good news about sincerity.

Here's the bad news:

If you say that you are interested in freedom and happiness, if you say you are committed to having great relationships, knowing how to apologize will not make a difference, unless you do the sitting nervously in a café. And even then, you've got to go through with the apology too, no matter how scared or embarrassed you are. You can't leave before the magic happens.

So, we think that the question of sincerity is answered by the process itself, in the same way that someone who exercises regularly will stay slim, whether or not that was their reason for exercising.

Of course, if you aren't going to be true to the promises you make in your apology, if you're waiting for a friend, just so you can apologize to them for something you've apologized for eight times before, you won't be thought of as sincere or truthful or anything good at all. As we've said, apologies lose their value if the promises we make are not kept. If you're apologizing for the same thing over and over, no matter how "expertly," *your apology becomes bullshit by definition.* It will be obvious to your friend that you are either a nut job, you just don't mean it, or both. Perhaps you are incapable of the kind of honesty and soul searching necessary for good relationships. Perhaps you'll never be free or happy. Is that you? Of course not.

As Step Five argues, you can't promise something you cannot achieve or have control over. For example, if you are not a morning person, don't promise to always attend a daily 7:30 a.m. meeting. Make a promise you can keep.

Don't ever promise something you think you can figure out later. For example, don't promise to make regular payments for a debt if you don't know where the money will come from. Never make promises you don't really mean (or that you don't think are important) just to look good or to slide on by, to make a "problem" go away. That will rob you of the very thing you are trying to attain.

PERFECTLY IMPERFECT

Many of us are loath to apologize because we fear being wrong and hate it when we are, even if we think we are just a little bit wrong. That fear and embarrassment is built on a secret expectation that we *should* be perfect, or even worse, that we *are* perfect, and we want to hide any glimmer that we aren't.

Hence, we are prisoners in our own jail, built from our own expectations of perfection, both our own perfection and our desperation that other people *should* be perfect. The door to this jail is wide open, but our fear makes us behave as if it is locked. In this cell, we are not free to apologize.

> We are all living in a fantasy of perfection.

Nobody's perfect. It's such a common expression that it's kind of a cliché. It's one of those phrases we say or hear so often that we rarely stop and consider its real implications on how we relate to ourselves. Nobody—not me, not you, not George Washington, not Mother Teresa, not The Princess of Wales nor The King of Siam is perfect. No one. However you define the word, no human being you know or have never heard of, dead or alive, historical or long forgotten, is or has ever been perfect.

You could, of course, invent a perfect person and write a book about them, but what would actually happen in that book? All good stories have a certain tension—some problem that needs to be solved. Something broken that needs to be fixed. Something or someone or some situation that is imperfect.

Or maybe the tension in your book would stem from your perfect person, interacting with an imperfect world, like an angel fallen from heaven. There are already books and movies that follow this kind of plot. Someone usually falls in love with the angel or makes the angel doubt his (her?) faith in some way and the angel is no longer perfect. Then, this crisis and drama eventually leads to some kind of unremarkable revelation like "love conquers all" or even . . . "Nobody's perfect."

We simply know the phrase "Nobody's perfect" to be true, even without a clear definition of the word "perfect." We know what we mean by "perfect," or at least we have the idea that we'll know it when we see it.

But what is it, this "perfection"? The Oxford English Dictionary is predictably nuanced in its definitions, but here are a couple, to get us all on the same page, if you will . . .

"Having all the required or desirable elements, qualities, or characteristics . . ."

Really? By whose standards? Desired or required by whom, exactly? To misquote another annoying cliché, "One man's croissant is another man's bagel" Surely this is just a question of *taste*—purely subjective.

Also: have you ever been someone or met anyone with *all* the required or desirable elements, qualities, or characteristics? No, you haven't, and even if you just met someone incredible and fell madly in love with them, how long till you notice a blemish or two?

> Another common definition of perfect is "free from any flaw or defect in condition or quality; faultless." Good luck with that!

So, when we think the people around us should behave in a certain way, this is, in effect, an expectation of perfection—a request or a hope that someone will live up to *our* definition of perfection. This is an expectation that deep down we know is impossible to achieve.

A common example we come across when working with colleagues and clients on their most important issues is the expectation that friends and family will know how they feel instinctively, without having to express it. How in the world could they possibly know that? They'd have to be mind-readers, and this is pure fantasy.

If our little phrase is true, and absolutely no one is, has been, or ever will be "perfect," however we define the word, then why do we still harbor the expectation of perfection in ourselves and especially others?

It could be that we're just trying to survive with our pants up, desperate not to be embarrassed, or maybe we're comparing ourselves favorably with others to feel good. It doesn't really matter. The point is that judging people for their "failings" is a lost cause. It's like sentencing yourself to be on a lifelong jury. And by the way, even if you think you have expressed clearly what you expect from people, who died and made *you* Pope? Is it possible that you have misread the situation? Or maybe more evidence is needed? Maybe you yourself are imperfect? You must be. *Nobody's* perfect.

Here's the thing: no matter how deeply we think we know that nobody's perfect, made it our mantra, had it tattooed on our body, we still judge people (including ourselves), places, and things to be "wrong." Shouldn't we know better by now? Luckily, it's not a question of knowing. It's a question of practice, out in the world.

Take a walk or a drive down a crowded street or visit a supermarket. Use public transport, or sit in a doctor's waiting room, or the DMV. Go anywhere, where (God forbid) you will inevitably see other people and notice the noise in your head. Some people say there's a "committee" in there; others refer to a single voice, but the commentary is much the same for everyone. "This person looks stupid, that person is sexy, another is ugly, and what is she wearing? He's old, she's enormous, they smell bad, or they smell good. This is taking too long, it's too hot or cold here, the chairs are uncomfortable, and I'm late or too early with a very good reason."

Reading our complaints here, we realize we sound like who we are, a couple of grumpy old Jewish guys; and you have your own style of inner conversation but it all amounts to the same thing: everyone judges everybody and everything constantly.

As Carl Jung said in his book *Flying Saucers*, "Thinking is difficult; therefore, let the herd pronounce judgment!"

You see, we actually know what you think, because we think it too. We all are 99% alike—science says so. That's the one thing you can fact-check in this book.

Not only are we mistake-making machines, but we are also judgment machines, and both are happening without any of our own volition. Some of those thoughts, if acted upon, would be terrible, illegal, unethical, or immoral. Thank goodness we have the choice not to follow all these thoughts with actions!

As we've said before, we are perfectly imperfect. Our friend Debbie once said "I wake up every morning knowing I'm going to make at least ten mistakes. No matter what I do, I'm going to make ten mistakes and knowing this, I don't have to worry or judge myself. I'm free."

When we aren't perfect, we have nothing to defend, and we are free to own our mistakes. We become free to apologize.

What a cause for celebration if ever there was one. You can retire from jury duty, pass the papal mitre on to someone more qualified to be Pontiff. Take your seat beside the rest of us.

Without a speck of dust, no raindrops or snowflakes are made. Without slight, accidental deviations in DNA, flora and fauna would not evolve to meet the needs of a changing environment.

The science philosopher Telmo Pievani writes, in his 2019 book, *Imperfection*:

> In the beginning, there was imperfection, which became the source of all things. Anomalies and asymmetries caused planets to take shape from the bubbling void and sent light into darkness. Life on earth is a catalog of accidents, alternatives, and errors that turned out to work quite well . . .

> The next time that you get caught up in a hunger for greatness and perfection, think of microbes: they were here before us, they chemically transformed the planet, we couldn't live without them, and everything suggests that they will continue to dominate the Earth even after *Homo sapiens* has left it.

Being one among many is the perfectly imperfect way to be, and don't misinterpret that and decide that you can't be amazing or extraordinary. Don't think that you can't stand out from the crowd at times. After all, everyone has things they are great at and other things they are not. Not only can you be extraordinary, but from this position as a perfectly imperfect person you will literally be anyone you want to be and achieve great things in your life for yourself and others—happy and free from the burden of useless weight of unfulfilled expectations and judgment.

So, let's have some fun and be useful before the microbes take over.

SPIRITUALITY

"If you're hungry, a ham sandwich is spiritual."

—Patti O

"I'm very spiritual… I just don't let it interfere with my daily life."

—Anonymous

Throughout this book, we have been clear about who we are and what we claim to know. We have also tried to carefully admit where we are not experts. Among other things, we may have mentioned that we're not, neither by trade nor training, psychologists, academics, therapists, anthropologists, philosophers, or even writers. To add to this list of what-we're-nots, let us now state for the record, in case you were wondering: we don't know anything much about God.

We have, however, been asked many times if we think there's a spiritual element to our thinking when it comes to apology. One friend said that we seem to be avoiding this question on purpose. We're not.

A simple fact: most, if not all, religions and cultures worldwide have some ritualized practice of apologizing, either to our fellow humans or to God(s), or both.

So, we thought, why not have a crack at (not) being theologians?

It's true that, for many years, Jason has regularly been a "Cantor/Soloist," a song-leader in synagogues and Jewish organizations. "Cantor/Soloist" is an unofficial term used to give a little clerical gravitas to an unaccredited position. He has led prayers at all services in the calendar, minor and major, and he has also sung in churches of various denominations. He's sung liturgy at many weddings, bar/bat mitzvahs, and funerals, and he is still available for yours.

Jason says: "I have loved the ritual of singing liturgy with a congregation since I was a kid. I have loved it and yet I have struggled with the meaning of it all. I have found great peace and community in the process.

The song lists haven't changed much for centuries, and the money is decent. But regardless, to let go and sing to the skies in a group is one of the greatest pleasures of my life.

Michael and I are yet to mention that we also are not archeologists, but having recently watched an eight-minute YouTube video on the subject, I can confidently tell you that human beings have been gathering together and singing in community for quite some time. There are many claims as to why that may be, some of which are universal and some specific to time and culture. I have no idea, frankly, if there is one spiritual, sensual, or neurological theory that can explain this phenomenon, but whether or not a deity is listening doesn't really seem to be the sole point of ritualized singing. No one has proved whether prayers are heard by God or not. God is silent on the subject. God, if you're reading this, with all due respect, some of us are growing rather impatient with your reticence."

And it doesn't take watching many YouTube videos on the subject to learn that people chat with God for many given reasons, and one very common one is to apologize in hope of forgiveness.

Catholicism has a tradition of "Contrition," in which the observer prays to God to apologize for their sins, which they often confess to a priest in advance. They then request forgiveness in return for the prayer. Protestant tradition says that sorrow for sin and acts of contrition are essential, but forgiveness is only attained by faith in the grace of God.

Judaism has its own approach to forgiveness from God, but prayers and acts of contrition, "Teshuvah" are mandatory, especially during the ten days from Rosh Hashanah (New Year) to Yom Kippur, the Day of Atonement. They are performed both in community and alone.

There's a Hindu and Buddhist concept, "Prāyaścitta," the Islamic "Tawba," or repentance. Shinto and other Animistic religions practice contrition and repentance in order to return balance and harmony to the natural world.

Of course, these extremely short references to ancient and often-complex ideas are hardly in-depth. If you're interested, we suggest further reading. Or a couple of YouTube videos. We're also not experts in comparative religion, but in one way or another, everyone seems to be at it, apologizing to God.

In this book we have written extensively of our evolving ideas about forgiveness, in the context of our practical program of apology that is designed solely to create Freedom and Happiness. We've been clear that Freedom and Happiness around our relationships with other people are our only goals when apologizing. They are both available even if after apologizing, your Friend doesn't forgive you. You are freer and happier for having taking responsibility for your mistakes.

It follows, naturally, that we don't apologize to anyone, including God, with *forgiveness* as our goal, let alone our expectation. Forgiveness is up to *them*, not us. Apologizing while expecting (or worse, craving) forgiveness is likely to backfire. In the case of God, some religions may seem to disagree with this view.

However it is expressed, the simple fact that acts of apology feature so universally in spiritual and religious practices is telling. Apology itself looks like something deeply human and begs the question, can we *be* fully human, or a spiritual being, having meaningful relationships, without seeing the value of making mistakes and cleaning them up? Perhaps, as Alexander Pope wrote, "to err is human, to forgive, divine." In other words, be real, make mistakes, be a mensch, and apologize—and leave your forgiveness to God.

Yet, so many of us have thrown away apologizing as a personal practice. Some see it as a weakness, a concession of not being the perfect person we want to portray. We sometimes see it as giving up the high ground or a position of power that we know will cost us in the future. After all, real men (or women) don't apologize, especially if they believe they are never wrong.

But the cost is our humanity, our spirituality, and perhaps even our relationship with God.

So far, we've demurred from using the word, "belief." This is because we unequivocally stress that you don't have to believe anything to get the most out of our ideas about apology, except perhaps that we're not lying when we write that our Six and a Half Steps has worked incredibly well for us and has given us Freedom and Happiness. This book is the recipe; our lives are the (let's say) pies. Not our greatest metaphor, but you get the point. You can't judge the pie by reading the recipe—you have to make the pie. Everyone likes a good pie.

As James, brother of Jesus, says in the New Testament, "Oh foolish man . . . faith without works is dead." (James 2:20, New King James Version). In other words, believe what you will, but take the steps.

Your humble writers' personal *beliefs* about God are for another day, but we will say this, with great certainty: when it comes to apologizing to God, why not? Can't hurt. It won't break our Golden Rule of not making shit worse, so have at it.

Our message is thus: whatever your tradition, culture, or religion, by all means perform whatever ritual, confession, contrition, prostration, or prayer you deem necessary to spur you on to authentically apologize to those people, down here on planet earth, that you have hurt. Make reparations where appropriate. Promise to be different going forward. Do the work of the Six and a Half Steps and carve out some freedom and some happiness for yourself, your nearest and dearest, and for the rest of humanity—no matter how many degrees of separation between us. The ripple effect may be infinite. It may be said to be divine.

HOW WE WROTE THE BOOK

"Two-fingered pecking at a laptop."

—Jason Feddy

"If I had known, I would have said 'no.'"

—Michael Waldman

As we've been writing this book, our friends and family have often asked us a couple of questions: 1) How did this book come about and 2) what does our process of writing look like? The background of these types of questions, we suspect, is that they are wondering, how did you two big egos manage to not kill each other? We felt it was worthwhile sharing with everyone how we developed our creative partnership.

Jason says:

Without getting into the sordid details of my, as some folks in 12-Step programs refer to it, "drunkalogue," when I say I was a heroin addict, your least-charming picture of what that looked like is probably about right. It wasn't pretty. To be clear and to avoid being romantic, I wasn't some kind of big-time criminal—I was a nuisance, and my life didn't work.

Once I'd managed to put a little distance between myself and drugs and booze of all kinds (as my brother likes to say, I wasn't a specialist, I was a pig), I began to follow the examples of the many amazing people I met in "the rooms." After all, some of them had lives about which I could only dream. Some of them even had jobs and friends! This meant taking those strange steps, often posted on the walls of meeting rooms the world over.

If you ask anyone in recovery what their favorite step is, and they resist the temptation to slip you the rather canonical answer, "I love them all," they're just as likely to say Step Six as they are Eleven, or Two, or any one of the dozen. For me, steps Eight and Nine were the steps that truly caused my head to explode. In a good way.

> Step 8: [We] made a list of all persons we had harmed and became willing to make amends to them all.
>
> Step 9: [We] made direct amends to such people wherever possible, except when to do so would injure them or others.

The drugs and the lifestyle that accompanied them had made me, like so many others, a very lonely chap. My family members, from parents to cousins close and distant, had all but given up on my ever getting clean. My friends and coworkers were beyond exhausted by my lies and broken promises, my self-aggrandizement and overly sensitive ego. I had a bag full of reasons for my life, none of which excused my anti-social behavior. I thought I could live without a ton of friends, but not my family. I missed them but couldn't see a way back into the fold.

So, even though back then I wouldn't have put it this way, it was my broken relationships that were making me feel that, drunk or sober, my life was a failure.

I wasn't sober very long before, with the help of others, I began to approach people I had harmed in the past, and began, in 12-Step parlance, to "make amends." The people to whom I owed something material (usually money) generally were pleased with receiving their due, no matter how tardy I was. My family, always forgiving and loving, though wary—they'd heard it all before—were just happy I was taking responsibility for my actions and the effects they had had on everyone.

The years rolled by. I mostly stayed sober and kept my promises. I learned and continue to learn the nuances of mending and amending broken relationships. My sense of freedom and happiness grew, and still grows as a result. Honestly, I must admit, I'm obsessed with tending to my relationships.

My childhood sweetheart Ava and I were married in 2010, and we built our nest in Southern California. We've stayed married by avoiding divorce, largely because when our relationship gets stuck, we quickly unstick it using the principles in this book. It's not perfectly smooth—once in a while we let off a little more steam than we'd like—but it works for us.

Ava and I met Michael and his wife Cindy at Laguna Beach Dog Park sometime around 2013. His foxhound rescue, Oliver, and our yappy poodle mix, Mrs. Pickles, became a kind of odd couple, and the six of us became friends.

Of course, Michael has a different story of how we met!

Circa 2015 I was thinking about how great it would be if there were a book about how to apologize effectively. I thought maybe I could write it, and I began to mention the idea to my friends. I realized early on that everyone seems to have an opinion about apologies, based on their experience (good, bad, or indifferent), their personality type, or whatever. Many, when asked, gave me a definition of apology that was quite different from mine. And the purposes of making apologies, as described to me, were strange and often self-centered. The title "The Glory of Groveling" was an early idea—I thought it was funny and would mildly irritate some people, perhaps just enough for them to pick it up off the shelf and see what it was all about. Mildly irritating people is probably not my best quality, but I do have a talent for it. I think I talked about the book idea a lot.

During the COVID pandemic, my friends and I would walk the beautiful trails that snake through the wilderness of Southern California. Not one among us is an athlete, but walking is healthy and it costs nothing. Usually, we'd walk five or six miles and then go for a guilt-free greasy breakfast.

This one morning, Mike and I were walking a trail in Aliso and Wood Canyons. I was waxing lyrical about *The Glory of Groveling*, when Michael, mildly irritated, stopped in his tracks and said, "When are you gonna write this fucking book?"

Good question, to which I replied, "Honestly I wouldn't know where to begin—I write songs, which are a half a page long. A book seems like such a massive undertaking."

Michael: "I'll write it with you."
Jason: "But you've never written a book, either."
Michael: "Right, but I know I could."

I didn't know whether my friend could or couldn't write a book, but I knew him well enough to know that if he committed to something, he'd show up as promised. The non-existent book I believed so passionately in wasn't going to write itself, and I'd done nothing (except yak on about it) to begin the process. I agreed to meet

Michael regularly and we began to work together, in person and remotely.

Collaborating on a writing project takes effort. I've co-written many songs and know the pitfalls. Of course, collaboration of any kind requires a partner—you can't collaborate with yourself, and relationships, as we know, can get stuck or break.

You need patience and good listening skills—knowing when to talk and when to shut your piehole. If you don't respect your collaborator's intellect, goals, and concerns, and believe in their good intentions toward you and the project, it's doomed. That may seem like a lot, but it's more common than you might think. And when (not if) you get stuck for any reason (usually with Mike and me it's because one or both of us is tired or hungry), then a good process for getting things back on track is essential. Take a breath.

As time has gone by, I'm sure Mike will agree, we've developed our own process that works really well for us. We're partners. I look forward to each session. I'll never forget Mike's words in the wilderness and once in a while I ask myself, "When are you gonna write the next fucking book?"

Michael Says:

Jason and Ava were two of the first people my wife Cindy and I met when we moved to Laguna Beach from Philadelphia. As a lover of live music, mostly retired and with plenty of time on my hands, I quickly found out that Jason was one of the most popular musicians in town. I would go see him play almost every week, and each time I would offer him something to eat or drink at the venue. Pro-tip: food is the way to Jason's heart.

At the time, Jason had a morning show at the local radio station, and he invited me in to hang out and chat while the music was playing. We soon found out we were both philosophical creatures with a strong sense of mischief making. From that point on, our families became close, and eleven years down the road, during COVID, Jason and I found ourselves taking a long socially distanced walk in the hills. I'm a little deaf, so our shouting echoed round the canyon.

But that is almost the end of the story. By this time, I had already started, run, and sold a very successful management consulting practice and before that I was senior manager and trainer for a global adult education company. When I left school, I taught children in the Philadelphia public school system, when I was just a child myself. As you can see, my life has been in the world of education.

When I met Jason, I had almost thirty-five years of working with individuals, couples, teams, and entire companies to make them better, more productive, and happier. The philosophy and methods I used to do so were introduced to me at Temple University and were deepened as I became a friend and colleague of the phenomenal Phenomenological Ontologist Werner Erhard.

Phenomenological Ontology, damn, that's a mouthful. Simply put, this philosophy claims if we can stop living in our story about our lives, and just deal with the cold-blooded facts, we get more productive and happier. Easier said than done, though. This perspective perfectly aligned with Jason's life experiences, so you can see this philosophy throughout our book together. The good news is our methods have the advantage of having worked successfully throughout the world in different cultures and for millions of people.

So, you got two guys, from different backgrounds and philosophical traditions, who recognized in each other some important similarities in their methodologies. We had both discovered through our own contemplation, trial, and error, that working and fulfilling relationships are central to the freedom and the happiness of human beings. By the way, researchers at Harvard University have been studying happiness since 1938, and in a recent article by study director Professor Robert Waldinger, MD., they concluded . . . you can't do it alone.

We both saw that the way to maintain those relationships was to face our own failings head on, and to take the time to find out what would work for others and ourselves, without blame, resentment, or recrimination. We had learned how to be adults in the world. Being human, we still fall off the horse, but we always try to get back on pretty fast.

The question now was, if we collaborated on a book (and really wrote it together as partners in crime) about what we'd learned, could the result be greater than the sum of its parts? Could it be more useful than just a telling of our two sets of experiences, lessons, and philosophical traditions?

Our first writing session was to set the stage. What did we want the book to accomplish for our readers and for ourselves? We offered each other what we called our "concerns for the book." By "concerns" we didn't mean our *worries* about the book, but rather what significant outcomes we each desired to fulfill by writing the book. We wound up with a short list that we agreed on for the project.

We then went on to address the more practical questions. How would we write? Where would we write? How would we edit what we wrote? This became our platform to stand on as we wrote together and it still is.

As we said, we had been good friends for over a decade, and now we were to become partners in a creative process, one that we hoped would become a business. This is a very different kind of relationship from the one we were used to. It would need, at the very least, a discussion.

And this new relationship, like any relationship, had to be a kind of compromise. As the eminent poet Mick Jagger wrote, (we) can't always get what (we) want. We are always asking, "What do you think?" and "Is that clear?" and "What do you/we/I mean by that?"

HOW TO LOSE A CO-AUTHOR IN 10 SECONDS

That's not to say we didn't have some brush-ups.

Michael's Apology to Jason

It was at our second writing session, in Jason's home studio, surrounded by guitars, microphones, and amplifiers, that our first major disagreement occurred. As often happens, when disagreements get really, really resolved, nobody can remember exactly what was said, but the following is my story and as the saying goes, I'm sticking with it.

At one point, in the middle of writing, Jason's wife Ava stuck her head in the door and offered her opinion on what she had heard us discussing. Jason listened to her and replied. What did he say? "Thanks Ava"

No big deal, right? In fact, very polite. Well not according to me. "Jason," I said, "I didn't agree to write this book with Ava and I'm certainly not going to ask her opinion on everything we write as we go along."

Now, add anger to the sentence above, plus stomping about, raising my voice, and being ready to storm out of the house. In other words, I had lost my shit. I had become mental and completely inappropriate to the situation.

Jason's reply was direct and bold. "I'm certainly not going to stop asking my wife for her opinion, and I'm definitely not going to stop considering her advice." I hated his response.

At the time I was insecure about my role in our new writing partnership, and I felt Ava would supplant my contribution. I was seeing red, my head was on fire, and I had now done the very thing I was afraid of. I had potentially sabotaged this new partnership.

Lucky for me, I could see all this, almost as a third person watching myself. After all, it wasn't the first time in life I had ever lost my cool. I could see what my fear and anger was costing me, and even though I still was angry, I swallowed my pride and apologized to both Jason and Ava. I didn't follow all of our steps but jumped right into "I'm an ass. You are right, and I apologize for putting you both in this situation." Being the generous and forgiving people they are, they said, "no problem, we just figured you were hungry or tired."

While we had already been friends for a decade, it was moments like this that forged our working relationship and gave us faith that an effective apology really does add freedom and happiness to life.

Years later, Jason told me, "It took me ten years of marriage to learn to listen properly to my wife. I certainly wasn't going to stop doing that for you!"

Jason's Apology to Michael

Michael and I are a team. This word "team," of course, is so overused as to have become a cliché. Maybe it would be better to use the term, *collaborators*. Collaborators leave their own personal desires behind to focus on a common goal, which, in the end, benefits them and creates something new—something that wouldn't have existed without the collaboration. This sounds easy, but it never works unless there's basic and early agreement between the parties involved. You have to be clear about values.

Michael and I are old friends, and now, we are business associates. We don't have a formal contract or agreement, but we have made a few promises to each other, and, as you know, we're pretty damn serious when it comes to promises. One promise Mike and I made to each other, when we had secured a publishing deal, was that we would not communicate with our new friends, the publishers, without talking to each other first. This was Mike's idea. He said that when communicating with them, we should always be "aligned." For one thing, it would ensure that we would always speak with one voice, creating clarity in our conversations with our publisher, and it would also mean that our private discussions would be ongoing, organic, and fruitful. I got it, and I agreed. I made a promise. Then I fucked up.

Here's what happened: Our lovely, hardworking, and supportive editor, Isaac, had written a description of our book, to be posted on online booksellers. It was really great. I showed it to a family member, who liked it, but who had one tiny criticism. She said we should change one word. I read the thing again and *wow*! She was right. It was such a small issue that I hadn't even noticed it, but now that I looked again, I agreed. That sentence would be made a little better if one tiny word was changed to another, different tiny word.

The next day, Mike came over to my place. He wasn't there in the capacity of my co-writer; he was coming with me as a friend to my gig at a beer garden, not far from home. While we were loading the car with guitars and speakers and such, I mentioned my conversation with my family member, about the one tiny word. Mike was happily moving stuff around in the trunk of the car and wasn't really listening. I became irritated and annoyed. I didn't say anything about it, but I decided to unilaterally let our editor know I wanted to make a change to his writing.

After my gig, I wrote to Isaac, and he made the change. I was happy. I cc'd Mike in the email and thought nothing more about it, until our next writing session, a video-call. I could tell immediately that Michael had something serious to discuss. He was gracious, but very clear. The agreement we had made about being aligned in all of our conversations with our publisher was very important to him. I had broken my promise to be attentive to it and he asked me to be very clear that I would never talk or write to them before he and I had had time to chat. He promised to do the same.

Now it was my turn to be annoyed. I felt trapped, embarrassed, and pissed off that I couldn't just do whatever I wanted. After all, I was a big boy! I'd tried to discuss the "tiny change" with Michael, while he was loading his car with my equipment and he'd brushed me aside. All the months of hard work and the joy of our discussion and writing and friendship disappeared as I became inflamed with self-righteous indignation. Oddly, I remember in some way observing myself doing this. Although I knew I was behaving badly toward my friend—I just couldn't stop myself.

Mike asked me to re-confirm our agreement. I petulantly said I didn't know if I could and that I'd need time to reconsider. Mike was calm, but adamant. He said that this was a deal breaker. He didn't want to continue writing until the agreement we had made was firmly back in place. He was ready to end the call.

This stopped me in my tracks. Was I going to jeopardize our book, and more importantly our friendship because of a feeling I had? I exhaled. Seriously, I felt myself re-enter my body! I took another breath. Michael's many years of experience in partnerships had taught him that this business of alignment was of crucial importance. In all our years of friendship and during our writing together, I'd never seen Michael take such a strong stand about anything. This was important. I put myself in his shoes. He'd seen something I hadn't, and he knew it was a red flag. I exhaled again. "You know what, Michael," I said, "you're right. I broke my promise to you and I'm sorry. I won't do it again. I'll make sure we talk about everything to do with the book and are aligned before discussing it with our publisher, or any other business associates, and I understand why. I could easily have undermined our relationship by bringing in a third party without your agreement."

We both relaxed. Michael smiled. He thanked me for my apology and for reaffirming our promise. We wrote for a couple of hours. I made a sandwich and walked the dog. Life went on.

By the way: alignment doesn't necessarily mean agreement. We may, in the future, disagree on this point or that word, or whatever, and we may need a professional, more experienced opinion, but we'll be aligned as to the need for that. Like a married couple who agree to the need for a counselor! This is not as weird a metaphor as you may think!

There's a significant point to be made here. The fact is that we have created a more fulfilling and resilient partnership in the process of writing a book on a subject that was already dear to our respective hearts. Maintaining and indeed increasing our love and respect for each other, while discussing a subject on which we were already highly opinionated, is testament, we believe, in the power of this process of apology.

Each time we approached a perceived impasse and our passions (if not our tempers) flared, we used this process to keep our relationship alive. As a result, both of us have abundantly increased our freedom and our happiness.

What does that freedom and happiness look like? Well, our friends and family, who know us better than we know ourselves, are correct: it was two big egos that set out on this journey together. We're not claiming that the process of writing this book has really changed that, but in the context of our relationship, we are able to focus on the book itself and not our feelings about it. Frankly, there's just less friction all round.

We take notes from each other freely and are happy to rethink each of our ideas in the best interest of the reader. We listen to each other better. We are better-humored about our own and each other's faults as we see them and we respect each other well enough to sense when it's OK to be frivolous and when to be serious. We trust each other to make things right if communication should break down.

Our experience of each other, and of writing the book, has been deepened and contributed to by the ideas of the book itself. Good thing really. If writing the book and diving into the world of apology didn't really improve our relationship, if we had fallen out over something small and couldn't recover, our book would be nonsense.

PERSONAL STORIES

What follows are examples of real-life apologies and examples of forgiveness—good, bad, and indifferent—from some of our friends and family members. They are written by them in their own words. We solicited these stories during the writing of our book, so no one had read the Six and a Half Steps before sending us their stories. We make no comment on them—we simply wanted to include some stories for you, the reader, to chew on, judge, to enjoy, or be repelled by. Hopefully you can relate to something here. We'd love to hear from you and to read your stories too. Perhaps we can include them in future editions. You can email us at: authors@gloryofgroveling.com.

David

I received an apology that I couldn't accept and I wouldn't accept, and I didn't accept!

I am an artist, who exhibits work at a major art festival in California. If there's one rule for artists in the show it is that no one encroaches into the display space of the artist next door. On this occasion, my neighbor did just that. I had built a wall, which was for my work only and the guy actually built his own display onto my wall without my permission. And he did this within forty-eight hours of the final inspection for the show.

He's got these two guys—they are building a wall onto the backside of my wall and they're pounding the devil out of my display. I said, "Well, you can't add onto my wall without my permission, so stop." The workers stopped and called the artist who they were building for.

When he arrived, I was on a ladder hanging my artwork. He looks up at me and says "Are you the guy that told my workers to stop? I'm from Chicago and we kill guys like you who get in our way." I was so astounded with this guy's moronic tone that I said to him "I'm from the Bronx and we eat guys like you for breakfast." He then pulled down his pants, mooned me in front of a crowd, said F-you, and walked off.

Our skirmish somehow got into the local paper, and so we were made to come before the festival board of directors. As a result, the other guy was put on probation for that year and eventually was excluded from the festival for a number of years. My actions to protect my booth were validated.

At one point, in front of the board of directors, he apologized to me. I wasn't really listening. I knew he was only doing so to get back into the festival. As such, I didn't think it was a real apology, and I didn't accept it.

George

She was an old friend from early in my recovery from addiction who, years ago, had taken a room at my house. She had a great sense of humor. We spent many hours laughing till nauseous. She was very beautiful, but the drugs had cost her dearly. I loved her, but not, "like that." She loved me "like that," but I pretended not to notice. I was just a boy who didn't know what to say.

Years later, and by sheer fluke, we bumped into each other. She happened to be working as a receptionist at the hotel where I was staying. Indulging my attempt to stay sober ("how cute"), she seemed happy to be close again. We sat in her car and I proudly started down my list of 9th Step amends. She had made the cut: I knew I had hurt her. I said, "I'm sorry I paid the rent late, sorry I pissed in the sink, sorry I left my dirty dishes, sorry I ate your pizza, sorry, sorry, sorry . . ."

Her calm resolve to listen soon disappeared. She grew increasingly agitated. I blindly plodded on till she could hold it no longer.

"STOP!!!" she reached across me and opened my door. "Get out," she shouted. "You don't get it! Take your little self-serving list and get out of my car. You have no idea how I feel, not then, not now! There's nothing real about your so-called amends. Get away from me. Just get out!"

How uncouth, I thought. I had so much more to reveal. She wanted none of it and she was right. My less than half-hearted attempt at amends only reopened her wounds and offered her no healing, no resolution. I had no idea what she felt, not then or now. I had made no real attempt to find out. I should have just said, nice to see you again, that would have been much better. Now she knows why she hates me. It wasn't unrequited love, I was an asshole, then and now.

Cody

I had the privilege of belonging to an elite military group in the US Air Force and, at the time of this story, I had been in special operations for about seven years.

The person in charge of our 8-man team was Captain X. He was well educated, could present himself well, but from the beginning I thought he lacked many of the leadership traits that I look for in commanding officers.

It started with a small, innocuous comment about how Captain X was not doing his job, followed by another small comment questioning his logic in decision-making, until all these innocent comments were built into a standard way of referring to him. Said plainly, what started out as observations turned into my talking shit about my commanding officer behind his back.

If I were on a larger team and only seeing the guy once a week, maybe I could have gotten away with that attitude and what I had said. But, when you're on a team of only eight guys, you're essentially living on top of each other, and any sort of friction between you and your other teammates has a great impact on performance—and that is noticeable.

One day, I realized that my relationship with Captain X had become extremely limited, and I felt constrained being around him, given what I had said behind his back. Looking back over the way I'd been, I soon realized that none of my behavior was making a positive impact on the team. I felt that the only way to move forward was to clear the air between us and to start over in our working relationship.

He was working in his office. I knocked on the door and asked if we could chat for a couple minutes. I started the conversation by letting him know that my commitment was to the effectiveness of the team and ultimately that was the most important thing for me. I then said "I want to apologize because I've been saying things behind your back that have not been positive. I've been gossiping about you and not talking directly to you. I'm sorry for doing that and I'm going to stop."

Captain X was a little taken aback by the statement. He said he didn't know I felt that way and that I should definitely come to him if there's anything that I see could be improved or changed in the way he's running the team. I don't think anybody had ever had such a straight interaction with him and apologized about something like this. There was new lightness in the room and a new level at which we could now communicate with each other. Our relationship after that moment was totally transformed. Now, neither of us were the crying type but I'm sure that he could also tell something had shifted in both me and him.

Henry

I work for a large American multinational company, and my work sometimes takes me abroad.

One time I was working in Vietnam for a few days. The schedule was busy and stressful, but one evening I found myself alone for dinner in a crowded restaurant at my hotel. Another company employee, Arthur from China, happened to be there at the same time. We decided to eat together.

As we got to know each other, we discovered that the two of us had similar interests, especially in our love of history and philosophy. We talked about many ideas and historical events—it was a great experience for me to hear first-hand the perspectives of someone from a background and a culture so different from my own.

At one point, I asked Arthur if he had read anything by the writer and historian, Yuval Noah Harari. I am inspired by him as a great academic, thinker, and speaker who has sold millions of books worldwide.

"Yes," replied Arthur, almost whispering, "But while I agree with many of his ideas, I cannot take him seriously. He is a homosexual."

I was taken aback. I told Arthur that my son is gay, and since statistically 10 percent of the world's population is gay, that means there's a good chance that 10 percent of the people in this restaurant are gay, and what's more, a similar percentage of Arthur's family is probably gay too.

Arthur was clearly unsettled by my remarks. He seemed flustered and slightly red faced. On reflection, I imagine that he was extremely offended by my comments, especially those about his family. My scant knowledge of Chinese culture suggests that he would have been extremely embarrassed by the loss of face I had caused him.

Anyway, I had no intention of ruining what had been a very pleasant evening by trying to change the beliefs of my new friend. We moved on, talked about other things, had dessert and said good night.

The next morning, back in the dining room, I bumped into Arthur. We sat opposite each other once again. "Hey, Arthur," I said. "I've been thinking about last night and wanted to thank you for a nice evening. I also want to apologize to you. I wish I hadn't mentioned your family, that was uncalled for and rude." Arthur seemed happy to hear my apology and he visibly relaxed.

After breakfast I took a cab to the airport. I left Vietnam and went home to my family. It was a successful trip on many levels. Good business, great food, nice people. It's a beautiful place to visit.

Bella

The following apology was made completely on WhatsApp.

Bella's sister Janet is married to Mark. Mark asked for Bella's suggestions for a birthday present for Janet. Bella recommended a particular kind of jacket, but then, as a result of miscommunication, unbeknownst to Mark, Bella bought that same jacket for Janet herself. Mark was upset.

Here's the conversation:

[7/7/25, 10:43:46 AM] Mark: Bella, I was dumbfounded, mad and hurt when a Sherpa jacket from Patagonia arrived from you for Janet for her birthday.

I was clear from our birthday phone conversation that the Sherpa jacket idea was something you gladly gave to me and I thanked you and told you I would pursue it.

While we looked at other jacket options for Janet in Denver, Janet and I never gave up hope on the Sherpa jacket possibility and were going to look in Patagonia when we got back to Dublin. We would have let you know if we had settled on and got a different jacket.

[7/7/25, 10:44:19 AM] Bella: Oh no !!!! 😱 Mark I get it! Thank you for telling me all this, I am so sorry! I definitely should've called you. What the hell was I thinking!? Not that this helps, but for what it's worth, when Janet was shopping with you and Michael, she told me that the kind of jacket she decided she wanted was a light rainproof windproof jacket that she could put over her other jackets. So I assumed that is what you were all going to continue to shop for and the Sherpa jacket idea was out the window. So in my mind over here, I thought well I'll just go ahead and get her the Sherpa jacket on this end. Again, I'm so sorry, I really thought things have changed over there and I should have called you about it. My apologies, really.

[7/7/25, 10:44:44 AM] Bella: If you'll let me make it up to you when you're ready, I promise I'll come up with an even better gift idea.

[7/7/25, 10:45:04 AM] Bella: PS, when you're ready, let me know if there's anything else that you need to hear from me. I'm sorry to have caused you even one moment of angst.

[7/7/25, 10:45:32 AM] Mark: Bella, just read this. You're being accountable for my upset means the world to me. Thank you for your listening. I will be in touch. I love you.

[7/7/25, 10:46:15 AM] Bella: I love you too Mark

DAVE

I once worked as an academic specialist physician at a prestigious university in the Northeast United States. Over a period of six months, I saw a patient a number of times who was suffering from severe and disabling symptoms. I pursued a long and complicated workup with multiple tests for her apparently unrelated issues. Ultimately, I came to the conclusion that she had no organic disease at all and was suffering from a psychosomatic condition. I referred her to a psychiatric colleague who was an expert in such disorders but on hearing my proposal the patient became very offended and stormed out of my office, apparently never to return.

Fast forward two years later, as I was leaving an examination room on my way to seeing a patient during a long day of appointments. I was approached by a woman who had been waiting outside my examination room. She introduced herself and asked me if I remembered her but I had no recollection of any prior encounters. She reminded me that she had been my patient and of her reaction to my diagnosis. She had come to town specifically to apologize for being rude and storming out of her last visit so long ago. It turned out that after some deep introspection, she did follow up and see a psychiatrist who concurred with my initial suspicions and after some intensive therapy, she had recovered completely.

That was a really welcome heartwarming apology. The clinical outcome was excellent and as a practicing physician with many years of experience, positive feedback like that, albeit relatively uncommon, is always welcome.

Sarah

The need for my youngest child to continue an extra hour of tutoring three times a week was obvious. He had been having trouble learning to read. It turned out he had a visual perceptual problem and that working with a reading specialist would greatly help him. He enjoyed his work with the tutor while improving his reading. It was a win-win.

Second grade was about to begin and I just assumed we would pick up with the three times a week tutoring as the school and the tutor had recommended it continue. And though it wasn't cheap, money was not a problem.

Christopher, my ex, decided the tutoring was not necessary and had notified the tutor that her services would no longer be needed.

As I picked up the phone to call him I was tense, mentally gearing up for a fight and steeling myself for the verbal abuse that was so often flung on the few occasions that he would actually engage in a conversation with me. I was also thinking of two moments in the past year that affected me powerfully.

The previous year I had been on something of a spiritual journey. I was exploring my faith, Judaism. Strangely I have ultimately turned away from faith, but that year I received a gift for my efforts.

That past April I had been at a discussion at a beautiful apartment in New York City. It was a blue sky day and the apartment had floor to ceiling windows overlooking Central Park. The trees were bursting with new life and as I was thinking about maybe a walk through the park, the lecturer's words pierced through, "you need to forgive those that are most difficult to forgive . . ." My immediate thought was *NO! FUCKING! WAY!! He doesn't deserve it!!*

I was stunned by the immediacy and the intensity of my reaction. Was I really that angry? I hadn't thought I was that angry. I sat with that anger. The speaker's words faded out again and I sat with my feelings.

Later that year in August I was continuing my spiritual quest. I was in Aspen, Colorado, on an early morning group hike with two rabbis. We were sitting on some rocks, there were twelve of us, in a circle. The holiday of Yom Kippur, the Jewish holiday of forgiveness, was almost upon us. We were discussing the ritual of fasting and Tashlich, the symbolic casting off of sins. I was again lulled by the physical beauty of the mountain and was not paying full attention when the rabbi said, "and what is most important is to forgive those that are the most difficult to forgive . . . ," almost word for word what I heard last April. But this time my thought was a big, huge *HOW???? How can I do that?*

With Yom Kippur fast approaching. I picked up the phone, dialed Christopher, and braced myself. It was one of his typical answers, "What do YOU want?" putting me immediately on the defensive. I took a breath and said, "Hello Christopher, how are you?" "Hi" he conceded, "What do you want?" I said, "We need to discuss the tutoring." He said "There is nothing to discuss. It is a crutch, you baby him, enough is enough." I said, "The school is still recommending it and it has really helped him with his reading."

He then went into a very long rant, disparaging me as a mother, our son as weak, we were both lazy and despicable. As he continued to babble, (and that's what it started to sound like, blah blah blah blah blah) I suddenly said, "CHRISTOPHER I FORGIVE YOU." Though I am not sure I yelled, it felt like I did.

He stopped a silent pause and then he said, "what?" I said, "I forgive you, you may not think you need to be forgiven but trust me, from my perspective I need to forgive you, and I do." Another pregnant silence, then, "Oh, thank you, well. . .goodbye then." I said "Goodbye." and placed the phone on the receiver.

I sat with it for moment and I realized a thousand pounds, a weight that I didn't even know was sitting there, rolled off my back. I felt light, lighter than I had in years. I also knew at that same moment that this didn't fix things, that somehow I was going to have to forgive him again and again and again. But that seemed OK.

I also realized we hadn't finished discussing the tutoring. But that also seemed OK. And to his credit, this one time, he paid for it, didn't interfere for that year and for the next few years until the school felt it was no longer necessary.

John

Nearly thirty years ago, a work colleague came to me after attending a well-known personal growth retreat and asked if we could speak privately. "Of course," I said without hesitation. I deeply respected this woman—her talents, her contributions to our team—and had even helped facilitate a unique arrangement that allowed her to work from home.

What she said next completely blindsided me. She told me she wanted to apologize. Over the past two years, she confessed, she had consistently undermined my leadership, turned people against me, and withheld support—all because she believed I had wronged a close friend of hers. I was stunned. I had no idea this had been happening. I had wondered why some things were not going well, and I had sensed certain undercurrents I couldn't quite explain, but I never imagined they stemmed from deliberate actions by someone I had supported and trusted.

In the moment of her confession, I could barely process what she had done, let alone her apology. Nevertheless, I accepted it. She asked if she could hug me, and I allowed it. As she walked away with tears in her eyes and a smile on her face, I stood there, boiling inside. The relationship and all my trust in her was shattered. I never wanted to see her again. I've done my best to ensure I have no further contact with her. Her apology may have unburdened her, but it has become a burden I still carry.

EXERCISES AND CHECKLIST

Now that you have read our entire book, perhaps you are ready to give yourself the gift of freedom and happiness by restoring a relationship with a dear Friend. Just so you don't have to go hunting through the book for what to do next, here are a couple exercises designed to help you get going, along with a complete checklist of our Six and a Half Steps.

APOLOGY EXERCISE #1: WHAT DID YOU DO?

FRIEND'S NAME

WHAT'S WRONG?

HOW DO YOU FEEL ABOUT IT? (HOW WERE YOU HURT)

ANY REGRETS?

WHAT DID YOU ACTUALLY DO/NOT DO?

APOLOGY EXERCISE #2: PUT YOURSELF IN THEIR SHOES

IMAGINE: HOW WHAT YOU DID AFFECTED THEM

IMAGINE: WHAT WOULD MAKE IT RIGHT FOR THEM

ARE YOU READY TO HEAR FROM THEM?

WHAT ARE YOU GOING TO DO NEXT?

THE SIX AND A HALF STEP APOLOGY CHECKLIST

STEP ONE: KNOW YOUR OWN MISTAKES

- ❑ I have a Fair Witness to support me.
- ❑ I know what I actually did, independent of my story about it.

STEP TWO: ASK PERMISSION TO APOLOGIZE

- ❑ I have privately forgiven my Friend for putting me in this situation.
- ❑ I have asked my Friend if it's OK to apologize to them.
- ❑ I have scheduled a time with my Friend to apologize.

STEP THREE: SAY "I AM REALLY SORRY".

- ❑ I know how I was "being."
- ❑ I said "I did X, I was being Y, I'm really sorry."
- ❑ I didn't give any excuses or reasons.

STEP FOUR: ADMIT THE IMPACT OF YOUR MISTAKES ON THEM

- ❑ I said how I imagined I affected them.
- ❑ I asked how I actually did affect them.
- ❑ I asked if there was anything more.

STEP FIVE: PROMISE YOU CAN BE TRUSTED IN THE FUTURE

- ❑ I have promised to be trustworthy and accountable.

STEP SIX: ASK IF YOU CAN DO ANYTHING ELSE

- ❑ I have asked "Is there anything else I can do to make this right with you?"
- ❑ I have made an appropriate promise in response.

STEP SIX AND A HALF: DON'T PUSH IT

- ❑ I have put aside my wants, needs and expectations for how my Friend should respond.
- ❑ I have given my friend the space to forgive, or not, in their own time.
- ❑ The Golden Rule: Don't Make Things Worse!

ACKNOWLEDGMENTS

In the writing of this, our first attempt at a book, we have many people to whom we owe our heartfelt gratitude.

Firstly, those generous friends and relatives who inspired us with their ideas, personal stories and recollections of apologies from their own lives, some of whom contributed directly to the text of the book: John Becknell, Lauren Simon, Sri Sundaram, Joanna Kleinman, Danny Sokel, George Boyer, David Milton, Amy Kalm, Cody Cerny, Viktoria Cerny, Dave Metz, and Michael Wainright.

To Zoom Rockman, our amazing illustrator, who found time to help us during a very busy time in his own career, and to his excellent, good humored and supportive family, Kate Lennard, Mark Garside and Ace Rockman.

To author Peter Block, whose initial support gave us the understanding that we had something of value, something worth reading.

To Rabbi Marcia Tilchin, her congregation and her family, whose trust and encouragement helped to begin this journey.

To those who gave us the opportunity and held our hand to a completed book: Terry Giles and Kalli O'Malley for their initial support and introduction to Skyhorse Publishing, our editor Isaac Morris for his consistently excellent suggestions, and to our publisher Tony Lyons for giving two greenhorns a shot at the big time.

Special recognition must go to philosopher and author Werner Erhard, whose ideas are often reflected in our writing. Additional, thanks to Werner and his partner Gonneke Spits for their wisdom, friendship and mentorship.

To the people at Landmark Worldwide for their dedication to have life be as satisfying and productive as possible. Thank you to Gina Donato especially, who read the book, gave feedback and navigated our way with the organization.

Many of the ideas in this book were also inspired by the work of Bill Wilson and Dr. Bob Smith and their writings. Special debts of gratitude are owed to Sheldon F., Larry Gill, George Boyer, Wendi Turner, Bob D., and the many, many great souls who have helped keep Jason sober and focused through the years. This book wouldn't have been possible without their expertise in making amends.

To the partners, colleagues and clients of High Performance Consulting and Insigniam for their support and their commitment to their employees.

To the many, many gracious people who have taken our calls and accepted our invitations to sit with us as we apologized for our crappy behavior. This book is, in part, dedicated to you. You have given us the most valuable gifts possible: Freedom and Happiness.

ATTRIBUTION

A number of the ideas in this book are those of Werner Erhard, and Landmark Worldwide, which owns the rights to and offers programs based on these ideas and other intellectual property, and are used in this book with the permission of Landmark Worldwide. The authors appreciate the opportunity to use these ideas. If you would like to participate further with these and additional ideas, you could consider participating in the programs offered at www.landmarkworldwide.com.